I love Betty Jean Robinson's new book. It will bless your soul.

—ORAL ROBERTS
*Founder of Oral Roberts Ministry
and Oral Roberts University*

Betty Jean Robinson is the highest, greatest gift God could give us on the earth—a perfect friend; a perfect, precious jewel.

—JAN CROUCH
*Cofounder of TBN Broadcasting Network and
hostess of the* PRAISE THE LORD *show*

Up on
Melody Mountain

Up on
Melody Mountain

Betty Jean Robinson

CREATION HOUSE

UP ON MELODY MOUNTAIN by Betty Jean Robinson
Published by Creation House
Strang Communications Company
600 Rinehart Road
Lake Mary, Florida 32746
Web site: http://www.creationhouse.com

Unless otherwise noted, all Scripture quotations
are from the King James Version of the Bible.

Scripture quotations marked NIV are from the Holy Bible,
New International Version. Copyright © 1973, 1978, 1984,
International Bible Society. Used by permission.

All songs and chapter titles in Up on Melody Mountain written by Betty
Jean Robinson and used by permission. All rights reserved by Melody
Mountain Music, Jehovah Jireh Publishing, and Opryland Music.

INTERIOR DESIGN: MARK MCGARRY

To my children, Rebecca Lynn and Elizabeth Kimberly, and to my grandchildren, Sunday, Joshua, Hadassah, Annie, and Rachel.

Contents ❧

foreword

When I think of you, Betty Jean Robinson, I think of Jesus! When I look into that precious face of yours, I can just see Jesus taking a handful of clay and molding a face that probably reminded Him of His own mother. I think He wanted eyes of love that can calm every fear you can have, a smile that warms the coldest heart, and a voice that would remind Him of what voices were really created for—to sing away our deepest hurts and make us whole again.

You are to me, Betty, the highest, greatest gift God could give us on the earth—a perfect friend—a perfect, precious jewel.

Betty, I know some of the troubles and trials you have been through; I hope you tell them all in this book so others can know that you can come out on the other side a perfectly honed jewel. Not scarred but *honed,* not beaten but *polished,* not broken but *smoothed*—every corner smoothed. You shine now like the glorious jewel God knew you would become.

If I could be like anyone in the world, it would be Betty Jean Robinson. I mean that with all my heart.

I remember a letter from a young man—a minister in a religious cult—who said, "I would tune in TBN, and when I saw the face of Betty Jean Robinson, I knew she had something I didn't have." And he gave his life to Jesus.

What you have is that precious Jesus face, that beautiful jeweled spirit, and we are all blessed because of it.

I love you.

—JAN CROUCH
SANTA ANA, CALIFORNIA

My Sweet Kentucky Home

I go back so many years in memory,
Scenes of childhood fill my eyes with tears,
So many years have passed since I've been gone,
But I'm still lonesome for my old Kentucky home.

I can still see Daddy plowing in the fields,
Smell the rain and hear the lonely whippoorwill;
Me and little sisters harmonize a song,
On the front porch of my old Kentucky home.

I can hear that old church bell ringing still,
As the saints sleep 'neath the cedars on the hill;
"Amazing Grace," across the mountains it would ring,
Wish I could shake their hands and sing with them again.

CHORUS:

Home, my home, sweet home,
Mama, sing me one more song
About home, my home, sweet home;
Carry me back to my old Kentucky home.
                    —BETTY JEAN ROBINSON, BMI

1

My Sweet Kentucky Home

They say I sang very early in my life. I'd sit on the front porch in a little rocking chair Pappy made, my pet "banty" rooster tucked under my arm, and I'd rock and sing, rock and sing, rock and sing. It must have looked comical. Sometimes a relative would teach me a song that was not considered nice by mountain standards, then ask me to sing it. I was always glad to sing, but I'd wonder why they'd gather 'round and laugh.

Most mountain people sing. In all the hills and hollows across the majestic Appalachian Mountains wherever we lived, the folks around us sang a rich variety of songs: bluegrass, ballads the old grandparents brought from Scotland and Ireland, native American songs, and of course the grand old hymns of the faith.

My earliest memories revolve around Pound Mill Hollow in Clay County, with its dirt roads and horses. Maybe once in two weeks an old rattletrap car would go by, and we'd all run out and look. It was something to watch, with its trail of dust from the dirt road floating behind it.

I can still see our two-room, hand-hewn log house set up there in the hollow, a beautiful place in summer, green with walnut and hickory nut trees, thick with blackberry and pawpaw bushes. Old wild roses and tall hollyhocks graced the yard, bare of grass and swept clean with a broom.

Back of the house in Pound Mill Hollow you went straight up the mountain. In front, an old ax leaned against the oak, hickory, and poplar logs stacked high on the porch, ready to supply the big stone fireplace where an iron cook pot hung from a rack.

A rock on the hearth was used to crack walnuts in the winter. Pappy would patiently pick out the nice kernels and feed them to us children. In an old iron stove in our lean-to kitchen, Mammy made the best biscuits in the world, big as saucers, thin and crusty. Nobody else could make biscuits that good.

Beautiful Anna Gray

This sweet Kentucky home lives in my heart, because that's where my daddy, General Dewey Rhodes (that was his proper name), brought me to live when he separated from my mother. I was just eleven months old and knew nothing about my parents' relationship except what they told me . . . a sad, sketchy little story, never fully explained.

My daddy married my mother, dark-eyed, beautiful Anna Gray from Leslie County, the prettiest woman around these parts, people have told me. Little Annie, just five feet tall and full of life, was way different from other mountain women. She was high-spirited, with sparkling black eyes and long, silky, black hair. She possessed the dramatic beauty an American Indian heritage often gives a woman.

Annie Gray played a guitar, which mountain folk didn't consider proper for a woman. She had a happy, free spirit, unlike the usual rigid behavior of other mountain women who had cut-and-dried ideas about how you should look, act, and be. I guess Annie, my mother, just didn't fit in.

Daddy could act very funny and humorous at times, but he was usually very reserved. His was a more rigid personality, but he was a wonderful, honest man, a hard-working man. I've heard people say that nobody could work like little Dewey Rhodes. He dug on those mountains. He helped build roads around those mountains.

My parents married very young. Soon afterward my mother wrote in her Bible, "He's gone to Hamilton, Ohio. I'm so lonely, and I don't know if he'll ever come back again." Young mountain men often went up North to Indiana, Michigan, or Ohio to find work to support their families; it was either that or work in the coal mines.

Whatever happened when he returned, I believe some of the old aunts disapproved of my little mother and got busy interfering in my parents' marriage.

Their relationship ended, and my parents separated. The big thing was, "Who's going to take Annie's baby, little Betty Jean?" The aunts influenced my grandparents, Pappy and Mammy Rhodes, that I ought to go with Daddy.

Life In Pound Mill Hollow

Gentle, happy, little Annie was so young—I guess the old aunts overpowered her. One day she rode a mule to Pappy and Mammy's house. One of my great-aunts went out and took this tiny baby—me—from my mother's arms. That was the last time I saw my mother.

Daddy took me to live with Mammy and Pappy in Pound Mill Hollow. His parents loved me and took care of me, and we stayed there until Mammy died. She was only fifty-five when she died of cancer after bearing twelve children at home without benefit of doctors. There were no doctors in Pound Mill Hollow, only missionary nurses who rode in on horseback to tend to expectant mothers and new babies. Here she was, suffering with cancer, and I was only three years old.

Mammy suffered alone. Sometimes she'd go up in the hayloft with her pain, maybe to cry, maybe to pray. She had a strong, overcoming faith. Mammy had been in that great move of God that came through, across this nation, when the heavenly dove flew into the mountains of Kentucky and brought the fire of the Holy Spirit to our people. Mammy had been in that movement, blessed by the Holy Ghost baptism with the evidence of speaking in tongues. That's how she became a little Pentecostal Holiness woman.

Mammy, a product of that great outpouring of God's Spirit which began in 1907 in our mountains and spread far, far into hidden hamlets and great cities alike, trusted God for everything, including, I'm sure, a miraculous healing of her body.

I don't know—I was too little to know. But I do remember climbing up in that hayloft to find her, where she retreated to endure her pain in the cool of the evening.

By now my daddy had married again, a little mountain girl from Bell County, over near Pineville in Cumberland Gap. Daddy had gone there to visit his oldest sister, Aunt Myrtle, who had married Uncle George Karloftis, a Greek immigrant who owned a fine restaurant, the Hub Grill, in the middle of Pineville. Uncle George, a short man with a thick accent, had stowed away on a ship to America when he was young and became so successful, even to opening a less fancy restaurant for Aunt Myrtle to run, that they could afford to have a maid.

Their maid was little Mahala Asher, just seventeen years old and a hard worker, and Daddy married her. He married Hala, as we called her, standing beside a bank where Preacher Garland pronounced them man and wife. (A bank, as we called it, was actually a hill-side.) Daddy brought her on back to Pound Mill Hollow, and she commenced to take care of me. Mammy loved Hala, and Hala loved Mammy. Young as Hala was, she took on a world of responsibilities, always worked hard, and was the cleanest woman I ever saw. Each afternoon she bathed me and dressed me in clean clothes, and I'd climb way up in the hayloft to show myself off to my Mammy.

"Mammy, ain't I pretty?" I asked.

"Yes, child, you are the prettiest little thing I ever seen," she said, as I lay down with her in the hay. I believe my little Holiness Mammy must have laid hands on me and gave me to Jesus, just as I have laid hands on my children and grandchildren and given them to Jesus. I believe the beginning of my life's dedication to the Lord came there in that hayloft through my Holiness Mammy.

My birth mother's father, Lee Gray, also had been touched by the Holy Ghost during that great move of God through our region. I never met Pappy Gray until after my little mother died at age forty, but I remember him as a tall, dignified man, his Indian blood very evident in his build and features, a man of God who preached on occasion.

On both sides of my family, relatives had "come into Holiness," as we described it, so I grew up acquainted with all this. Some of my relatives died speaking in the Holy Ghost, and people around them couldn't understand the strange words they spoke on their deathbeds . . . saints speaking in heavenly tongues.

Mountain people made much of a person's death experience. They built their kinfolks' caskets, laid them out, and dressed the dead. The wake lasted three days, with people standing beside the casket, preaching, singing, mourning, praying, and giving vent to grief as mountain people do. The sounds of their wailing and weeping could make chills go over you. Death was an awesome event to the mountain people.

They buried Mammy on a hillside near Redbird River under a big cedar tree. You had to ford the river in a wagon or an old truck, or find a low place and wade across in the summer. There were no roads, no cars, and no man-made noise. It is so beautiful there among the tall walnut, hickory nut, and pawpaw trees. In autumn the scarlet and golden leaves float lazily down the Redbird River and the sun sparkles on the water. There is no sound except for the wind, the river, and the songs of countless birds.

Up the Creek to Redbird River

After Mammy died we moved just up the creek to John Henry Revis's two-room white frame house set up on Redbird River. Daddy began working Dewey Langdon's place. Dewey Langdon was a schoolteacher who lived miles from us, and Daddy had to walk there and back each day to take care of his sheep and raise his tobacco.

My daddy worked like a mule: There was nothing he wouldn't do. He loved the land, loved nature, loved to improve the ground. Daddy would worm tobacco, flipping those old tobacco worms off and killing them, for fifty cents a day. By the time he fed Dewey Langdon's cows and sheep, took care of them, and walked the miles back home, it would be after dark when he came in.

One day Daddy came home excited. "I spotted a big beehive in an old holler tree and it's full of honey," he said. "Good white honey." That was the kind we liked, that special clear honey. "I'm going to raid it," Daddy promised. One day he put a piece of screen wire over his head to protect himself, set off for the tree, and came back home with a big bucket of honey dripping from long, plump honeycombs.

We were so happy we jumped up and down. What a joy! How we appreciated the things we had— our little Jersey cow and her yellow butter, a pig in the yard, a few chickens. The joy of those fresh eggs, or of leaving "settin'" eggs under the hen to hatch into baby chicks. We took charcoal pencils and colored our "settin'" eggs to keep from taking them to eat. We called them "diddlers," pretty little chicks that followed Daddy as he did spring plowing, getting worms behind his plow.

We worked with nature, and nature worked with us, as God intended. On a foggy or drizzly winter morning, Daddy knew the squirrels would come out, so he'd take his .22 caliber rifle into the woods and come back off the mountain with a string of squirrels hanging over his shoulder for a big pot of squirrel dumplings. That meat and gravy tasted wonderful during winters when we didn't have chicken to cook.

At Christmastime Daddy would sink a fish basket, one he had made out of chicken wire, with a big hunk of cornbread in it. He would sink it deep to the bottom of Redbird River. Perch, and even sun grannies and catfish would get stuck in there, and they tasted so good. We ground our own cornmeal from the corn we raised, grew potatoes, onions, and cabbage to carry us through the winter, strung greenbeans we called "leather britches," and hung them on the kitchen wall to dry. There was nothing better than the smell of a pot of wintertime dried beans, flavored with our home-cured fatback. I still dry those beans and cook them like that today.

That was life on the Redbird River. I left my childhood there. By the time I was three I had lost my mother and then my mammy . . . heartbreaking experiences for a baby.

My stepmother Hala, however, had endured lifelong drudgery and endless work, always more work, before she came under my mammy's loving influence. Losing Mammy may have been even harder on Hala than it was on me. She now had all the responsibility, with no loving older woman to advise and help her, nobody to encourage her in her lonely labors.

And the babies came, one after another. First Lucy Mae, then tow-headed George, dimpled Martha Belle, and finally little Shirley Ruth. I loved my little half sisters and half brother, but I had a lot of extra duties thrust on me very early. Hala couldn't do it all, and I was the big sister. Both of us looked after babies and toddlers every minute, it seemed like.

I started school there on Redbird River, a one-room schoolhouse that was also used as a church. I remember Daddy carrying me on his back down to the school when the snow was on the ground. We had no car of course, and usually not even a horse. Daddy loved a fine horse, dreamed about horses the way young men today dream of sports cars. But lacking those luxuries, all of us children can remember plenty of times when our daddy carried us through snow, rocks, briars, or floodwaters, clinging to his strong back. I love my daddy and cherish those memories of all he did for us.

The Songs of the Hills

Those days, those precious days of my early childhood, Hala and I would sit on the porch some late afternoons. How quiet it was—not a sound of a car or anything else—but if you listened real hard, if you were real quiet, you could hear the train go by twenty miles away. Twenty miles is like two hundred miles in the mountains, over those awesome hills.

We'd get real quiet and listen for the whistle. Hala would say, "Lord, there goes the train. I can hear it." There were people going by, so far, far away from us. I pictured the people sitting in that train. Then we'd harmonize, my stepmother and I, singing, "A long steel rail and a short crosstie. I'm on my way back home."

Or we'd sing in harmony, "The longest train I ever saw went down that Georgia line. The engine passed at six o'clock and the cab went by at nine." We'd sing other old mountain songs like "Barbara Allen" and "Little Bessie"—the songs our people brought from Scotland, Ireland, and England.

Songs wound through those mountains like that faraway railroad track, a never-ending stream of music. We sang songs of love and pain, tragedy and faith, stories and fun. Mountain people always sing full-voice, stomping out the rhythm with a workboot, emphasizing the distinctive, vigorous rhythm, the non-stop tempos, and close harmony. And if you were blessed, a fiddle or guitar would back you up.

Our songs kept us going. Music helps you bear the unbearable and celebrate all that's good. It became part of my blood. It's my heritage and my gift.

Daddy's guitar and Hala's singing set the rhythm and tempo of those early years in the Cumberlands, down by the old Redbird River, there where you could lift your eyes unto the hills. God used my father and stepmother, and so many other song-loving saints, to set my feet on the path where He wanted me to go. I love them all.

Livin' Up on the Mountain

I'm a'livin' up on the mountain and I'm alright,
I'm a'livin' up on the mountain and I'm alright;
Oh you don't have to worry, you don't have to get uptight.
'Cause I'm a'livin' up on the mountain, and I'm alright.
                                        —BETTY JEAN ROBINSON

2

Livin' Up on the Mountain

Daddy walked way, way across the field to Becky Gilbert's house where they had a battery radio, and he could hear the news. Directly, he walked back home where all of us waited for him on the front porch. "Well, they've started a war," Daddy announced. "President Roosevelt has started a war with Japan."

Daddy called it "Jay-Pan;" told us they'd killed a bunch of our boys, an awesome thought. Those days our communications were limited. There were no newspapers and no radio or electricity. An old man would ride a horse and bring our mail, if we had any, maybe once a week. We seldom got mail, but sometimes the old man brought news. That's how we learned that World War II was coming.

Mammy's Spiritual Legacy

I was little, but I remember. Our country was at war. Mammy was dead, and nobody in our house knew God the way she did. Mammy was a little Holiness woman, so full of love. Pappy, who mostly lived with us except when he visited his other sons and daughters, was a hard-shell Baptist and a good believer. My daddy was a good man, but not a committed Christian. Whenever he went to church, however, he'd find the poorest family and invite them home. We were poor, but he had a heart for those who were even poorer. We'd hurry home, and Hala would catch a chicken, wring its neck, and we'd pluck it, cut it up, and fry it. Lucy Mae and I would run out and dig potatoes and onions, and we'd have a big dinner. Daddy always believed in feeding the hungry.

Maybe that's because Mammy always fed the little poor children who showed up at her house hungry. They'd stand outside our paling fence—(picket fence)—and stick their little jars through so Mammy could pour a little buttermilk or sweet milk for them to drink. She barely had enough milk for her own large family, but she always shared.

Well, my old, selfish great-aunt told Mammy she had no right to give her own children's milk to "them pore old children whose daddy don't work."

"Things are sca'ce," my great-aunt said. She put a guilt trip on Mammy, and next time those children came back Mammy hollered out there, knowing it was wrong, wanting to share, "Children, I ain't got no milk for you today."

Livin' Up on the Mountain

As the little ragged boys turned and began to walk away, Mammy couldn't stand it. "Come back! I do have some milk," she called. I believe that as she filled those little empty jars with milk her own children needed so bad, dividing what she had, she set God's continual blessings into the lives of me and all her other offspring.

That little grandmother Mammy of mine knew the Lord says, "Give, and it shall be given unto you; good measure, pressed down, and shaken together, and running over, shall men give into your bosom."[1] I know that as for us, Daddy's children, we got awful low on food during some hard, hard times, but we never went hungry. God honored my Mammy's obedience.

That same old great-aunt who told Mammy not to give her milk to the poor children had plenty of buttermilk herself, but wouldn't give any away. She fed it to this huge hog she was fattening in a flooring pen, feeding it nothing but the best until it would reach two hundred pounds and be slaughtered.

When those poor children came seeking her buttermilk she told them, "I ain't got no milk today. You'uns go on up that road. I ain't got no milk." I can still see her in my mind's eye, a skinny mountain woman with a little bun of white hair, her apron reaching almost to her high-top shoes.

Daddy recalled one time when he saw her send the little children on, and then she immediately slopped a gallon of fresh, warm buttermilk into the hog trough. Daddy said that "big fatten" hog squealed, jumped straight up in the air, and fell stone dead!

We believed the Lord did that—took the most

valuable thing she had, her biggest hog. Mammy had taught us that if we hold something to ourselves we will lose it. Our very soul and spirit will shrivel, and we will set curses before our children rather than blessings.

I thank God for Mammy and Pappy. My little Holiness Mammy had Jesus in her heart, and walked what they called a "Holiness walk." When you walk with Jesus your heart stays open and you give freely, as Jesus gave.

Little George and the Watermelon Seeds

Mammy's spiritual legacy fell on us in an unforgettable way soon after we moved into John Henry Revis's house, where we lived when war broke out. It was springtime, and the cow already had her calf, a little heifer. That meant we'd have another cow to give us good milk and sweet butter, which always made us glad.

The March wind blew big fluffy clouds across a brilliant blue sky, making us all eager to plow the fields and get the onions and potatoes in the ground. We didn't think of it as work, because planting meant food. Happy times were when the garden, orchards, cows, hogs, and everything else produced as they were meant to do, and there was an abundance in winter.

One of Becky Gilbert's people, Ethel Howard, who lived across Redbird River, came over and wanted to trade some garden seeds. Hala, my stepmother, had laid the seeds out on the bed and was counting them out when I came flying into the house yelling, "The calf's out in the garden!" Hala ran to pen it back up.

Livin' Up on the Mountain

As we all rushed out to help corner the calf, little George, my pretty little blond half-brother, then a toddler, got into the watermelon seeds. Seeds were so scarce that when we divided them with our neighbors we counted them. He commenced to cry and cry and cry, and even after Hala rushed back into the house, he still cried.

Day after day, that baby cried, and it seemed like it got harder and harder for him to breathe. Sometimes he almost choked. The doctor lived miles away, but daddy got on his old mule and rode away up the creek to fetch him.

"You've got to take this child to the hospital," the doctor told us. Daddy knew he would have to sell our cow to do so, because we had no money. It's an absolute tragedy to sell a cow, but Daddy knew he had to. He and Hala sat in the front seat of the old truck, Hala holding the sick, crying baby, and the rest of us rode in back. We took George to the hospital.

After several days, during which nobody could find out what was wrong with little George, Hala declared she was taking him home. "You can't take your baby out of the hospital without a doctor's permission," the nurses told her, but Hala said, "You just watch me! This is my baby, and you ain't doing anything fer him. He's a-dying, and I'm taking him out."

Hala brought little George, sicker than ever, back home. The old doctor told Daddy, "Dewey, the baby's going to die; he can't breathe. I can't do anything, because I don't know what to do, but I can tell you where to take him."

He told Daddy about a children's hospital in

Louisville, Kentucky, and offered to find a way to get him admitted there. "I know you have no money," he told Daddy, "but the name is *Children's Mercy Hospital*, and they are known for their mercy. They will take him."

Daddy took Hala to Manchester, and she took the baby on the bus to Louisville. By then little George couldn't drink his milk, because he'd choke when he tried to do so. He couldn't swallow a thing. As Hala tried to breast-feed her baby, that pretty, white-haired little boy was choking, his eyes rolling back in his head, turning blue around his mouth. His lungs rattled.

Hala must have been frantic. She knew her child was at death's door as she approached that hospital. She knew how proud Daddy was of his only son, how terrified that he might lose him.

The hospital admitted them and immediately started treatment, using modern procedures. They x-rayed the baby, ran a probe into his lung, and immediately found the obstruction. A watermelon seed that had sprouted in his moist, warm little lungs actually was cutting off his breath. They removed that sprouting watermelon seed from the lung—a miracle!

The next morning Hala watched her son sucking milk greedily from a bottle. He was happy, hungry, the color back in his cheeks. What joy for all of us when she brought him back home, and what a miracle of God.

Moonshine Miracle

You might think a happening like that would turn a

man to the Lord, but it was not that way. Daddy knew about the Lord, but he did not *walk with* the Lord. He was a good man, a man who respected his own mother's Holiness and his daddy's Baptist beliefs, but he hadn't committed his own life yet.

In our living room, where we had two beds, an old trunk, and little pieces of starched white sheets at the windows for curtains, someone had driven a nail into the old rose-patterned wallpaper and hung a sign, a little colored cardboard sign with sparkles on it, that said "Jesus Saves." Another nearby sign said, "Jesus Is Coming Soon." But we didn't pray, and we seldom went to church.

The beautiful land, good crops, plenty of hard work, and his growing family seemed to satisfy my daddy's soul. Though he worked from dawn to dusk destroying those old tobacco worms, he never complained. We moved to Sugar Creek.

Then came a Saturday when old man Gibson came from way far in the hollow and asked Daddy to go with him. The old man made moonshine, and for some reason Daddy went with him and drank some of that 'shine. He was gone a day and a half, probably passed out. He came down off that mountain at night and went straight to bed, and oh, dear God, we heard the most awful sounds in the middle of the night.

Daddy had convulsions, one after another. Hala told me to run get Dewey Langdon because he could get us to the hospital in Bell County, where Aunt Myrtle lived.

Dewey Langdon lived way across the rolling

meadows. I was a frail seven-year-old. At two in the morning, the moon bright as a lantern, I raced through woods and fields. I could hear foxes barking in the hills, but I wasn't afraid of anything in the wild, or even of Mr. Langdon's mean dogs. The only thing that scared me was his old buck sheep, asleep in the barn that I'd have to cut through in order to cross the meadow behind it. *If I wake that sheep he'll chase me, and I won't get across that fence in time to get help for Daddy. . . .* I tiptoed through that barn, and—thank You, Jesus—that old buck sheep never woke up. I woke Mr. Langdon and urged him to hurry. He seemed to take forever, just putting on his shoes while I silently thought, *My Daddy is dying. Please hurry up!*

We headed out. After we got back home and carried Daddy to Mr. Langdon's truck, we went to Bell County, and on to Pineville Community Hospital. We left everything as it was at home, and took our dear daddy to the hospital because we thought he was dying. One convulsion after another shook his body—eight in all—and the doctors said he had poisoned his system so badly that he'd have to take medication the rest of his life.

Daddy almost didn't make it; he was hospitalized for several days. As he slowly recovered, we decided we'd better stay in Pineville. Aunt Myrtle gave Daddy a job washing dishes in her restaurant and raising hogs for the meat her business needed. I reckon we embarrassed Aunt Myrtle, we were so ragged and poor. She never wanted us to come into her restaurant, but Uncle George didn't care. He'd invite us to eat in his grill with its pretty tablecloths and lawyers and judges sitting at various tables. Uncle George would ask us what we wanted. He knew we liked his homemade doughnuts, thick hamburgers, and delicious ice-cold milk. Sometimes he would give us a Coca-Cola, because we never had anything like Coca-Cola otherwise.

Pappy, with his old brogans and bib overalls, especially embarrassed Aunt Myrtle. He'd walk through the place from the front door to the kitchen, where he knew the black cooks had saved chicken gizzards to fry for him. He loved those cooks and they loved him, and they'd fry those gizzards just for him. Aunt Myrtle always asked Pappy who was her father, "Why do you always come through the front door? Why can't you use the back door?"

Big-hearted Uncle George understood that we felt insecure, poor, and unworthy. He knew that when we sat at his fine table we felt like we were good as anybody else. It was special. Daddy named our little brother George after this good Greek-American uncle.

Eventually we returned home to Redbird River to gather our things and move. We had a smokehouse full of hams, a hundred-pound can of rendered lard, a hundred-pound can of molasses. We also had sweet potatoes, rolled separately in brown paper pokes so they'd keep, and plenty of canned goods. Shuck beans, "leather britches," hung around the kitchen wall. We had a wonderful fullness of home-grown provisions.

We went back for all that, plus our two old beds, our trunk, dresser, cookstove, the long, homemade wood kitchen table, old cane-bottom chairs, wash pans and kettles. We put all that in the truck, then went out to the smokehouse to get the hams and other provisions.

It was empty! We were so poor and daddy so sick, yet someone—some people said it was one of those men who wouldn't work and whose children always came begging for milk—took all we had. I don't know whatever happened to those children's daddy, but I know he didn't plant good seeds for them. I'm sure that man never prospered after that.

If you take, it will be taken from you; give, and it will be given to you. It's just as simple as that. The Lord is good, and He is righteous. His promises are "yea and amen," but He won't put up with things that are not right. He is a holy God, and I pitied that man's little children.

Whether we realized it or not, our family had experienced still another miracle of God. Daddy was weak, poor, and still sick, but he was alive. Hala and me, with my two little half-sisters and half-brother, squeezed into that loaded truck and headed for Bell County to begin our new life in Pineville.

I don't know if we hoped for anything; we just went. We didn't know that my Holiness Mammy's faithful God also went with us to Pineville, where there were to be even more difficulties and trials.

But God was surely there. I was on my way to meet Him.

Endnotes
1. See Luke 6:38.

Daddy's Song

I have so many memories of Daddy and home,
Though it's been a long time since I've been gone.
One thing I've noticed as I go down the line,
There just ain't no Daddy like this daddy of mine.

He loved the little children, loved the man on the street.
He gave them bread from our table, he'd give the shoes off
    his feet.
So simple in his country ways, there's so few of his kind;
There just ain't no Daddy like this daddy of mine.
        —BETTY JEAN ROBINSON, ASCAP

3

Daddy's Song

Ol' Straight Creek, where we moved so Daddy and us could start over, turned out to be an interesting place. This was the county seat, with a big courthouse in the middle of town and a huge chained rock they claimed would otherwise fall down on the city. We were in coal-mining country, and on Saturdays the miners and their families streamed into town.

The preachers came too, and stood at separate corners of the courthouse square preaching the gospel. The Holiness people, Pentecostal folks, had a preacher on one corner, and the Baptists held down the opposite spot. They all preached at the same time, full force, to crowds arriving to shop at Newbury's Five and Dime or have a hotdog and Coke at the ice-cream shop.

The men of God preached every Saturday, yes Lord! Many heard the gospel, and a conviction fell on those old coal miners. They'd kneel right there in that courthouse square and ask Jesus to come into their life.

The Pentecostals' corner of the square was always full, with lots of singing, shouting, and praising God. The good old Baptists preached the cross; the Pentecostals preached the cross *and* the baptism of the Holy Spirit with the evidence of speaking in tongues.

Of course, we had our snake-handlers too. Those who took up serpents, they were called. They were good people, and I noticed others seemed afraid to say anything against them, because they showed such love, and wore such sweet countenances. You've got to walk a straight walk, walk a good walk, walk with real faith if you're going to pick up one of those rattlesnakes fresh out of the mountains.

Hard Times at Straight Creek

Daddy got us a little house at Straight Creek by the railroad tracks, a house set up on rocks. It set by the branch of the creek, and oh, that good cold water. I'd go to sleep at night hearing that mountain water running out under the railroad trestle and down the branch . . . a lullaby sound as it gurgled over the rocks.

Soon Hala was expecting another baby, so Daddy went north to find work. He had to make more money, and Pineville offered nothing better than the coal mines. So Pappy stayed with Hala and us while Daddy, like so many other poor mountain men, left his family and went to Detroit to make cars.

This was wartime, and Daddy had tried to enlist, but he was a little overage and had all those dependents. Sometimes when we'd buy a newspaper the headlines were so grim. People were highly patriotic in those days, everyone was so proud of our boys that we'd sent to help defend our nation. Our country was in trouble, the world was in danger, and those strong, young mountain men, so handsome in their uniforms, went off to protect America. Daddy hated that he could not do his part.

There was a war civilians had to fight, too; women with their ration-stamp books, men building vehicles and ships. Daddy went to Baltimore to build war ships at Bethlehem Steel's shipyard. He was a smart man, mostly self-educated, full of common sense though he had only a fifth-grade education.

When Daddy could he moved there and sent for us to join him . . . The government had slapped together some housing for the folks who were moving out of the mountains to build those ships, so we left Straight Creek, got on a train packed with soldiers, and went to Baltimore.

Mountain Folk in a Foreign Place

This was a land we knew nothing about. The school teachers looked down on us little mountain children who didn't have warm clothes against the cold winds blowing off Chesapeake Bay. Us little briar-hoppers, the hillbilly children, really suffered there. We were laughed at and mocked, so we huddled together and kept to ourselves. That was my first encounter with the cruelty of prejudice.

One day—hallelujah!—the war suddenly ended. Oh, victory for America! How happy everybody was. Every church bell in Baltimore was ringing, ringing, ringing. The war was over . . . and so were America's years of sadness, sacrifice, weariness, and tears.

Daddy's job was over too. With bells ringing, factory whistles blowing, hillbillies were leaving there as fast as they could in their loaded-up cars and old trucks, heading back home. We threw our beds and cookstove into an old truck and began the twenty-hour drive to Straight Creek, us kids in the back with our belongings and Hala up front, holding our baby, Shirley Ruth.

Flooded Out

We had leased our house in Straight Creek to someone else for a year, so we couldn't go there. Like the other mountain people returning home, we needed some place to stay and somewhere for Daddy to work. Neither seemed possible to find. After a desperate search, Daddy finally located a tiny house beside a creek in Carey, Kentucky. Made of crossties daubed together with creek mud, the one-room house with two lean-to rooms sat almost on the railroad track. With the creek on one side, the railroad track on the other, we had to cross the track to get to the outhouse.

Daddy's Song

Since we'd dealt with floods in the past, Daddy made sure to ask about that possibility. The lady who rented to us said there had been no floods in the past, and we believed her.

We nearly starved. The rocky ground yielded a poor garden. Daddy could not find work, and sometimes we had nothing to eat but milk poured over macaroni and water gravy over our breakfast biscuits. Daddy hardly knew what to do. He got so desperate he went up in the mountains that summer and picked blackberries for Hala to can.

One night a strange sound awakened my stepmother. Fruit jars were bumping together in the lower end of the lean-to, and as she jumped out of bed she realized that water was rising around the house. There was no electricity, and when night covers that mountain it gets dark—pitch dark! We hurried to do what little you can do when floods come—turned the bedsteads on end against the wall, piled the mattresses high, and hoped the water wouldn't rise that far.

When Daddy opened the front door, water surrounded the house. The rear of the place stood high on posts, but the front door was close to the ground. Six old chickens huddled in a corner of the high part of the house squawking loudly. Daddy felt sorry for them, so he grabbed an ax, chopped a hole in the wall, and flung them out over the fence to run wild.

At last Daddy waded out into that watery blackness and carried us, one by one, to higher ground. We walked miles down the railroad track to the home of the lady who rented to us and crowded in with her until the waters went down. Later we moved back to the place before the old logs really dried out, and little Shirley Ruth caught scarlet fever from exposure to the polluted waters.

Hala Grieves

Daddy and the rest of us endured. I walked the railroad track to school every day. The house dried out and they cleaned the rusty cookstove by rubbing it down with a greasy meat skin. Things gradually became somewhat normal, except that we never went to church. Daddy either didn't know or wouldn't talk about God, and we never prayed. Seemed like we didn't have time for God, with everyone working so hard just trying to get by.

One day when Daddy and Hala left to pick blackberries, we had nothing in the house to eat except crackers and jam. They left me in charge of my two-year-old sister; I was bathing her in the washtub in the kitchen. She loved that water so much she got back in the tub again, so I got her back out, dried, and dressed her in her feed-sack bloomers, then fed her her crackers and jam. I couldn't have known that this was the last time I would feed my little sister on this earth.

When Daddy and Hala came down off the mountain we all got busy. Since we had no refrigerator we had to can the blackberries immediately. One person had to chop stovewood and start a fire, another stemmed and cleaned the berries, and my little sister Lucy Mae carried a quart of buttermilk to the neighbors up the railroad track to sell for a quarter. Each had a chore to do.

Somehow little Shirley Ruth discovered the gate had been left open a crack, and she got out. Soon we missed the baby and began to search high and low, under the house, out in the dirt, then toward the creek and the railroad track. She loved for us to try to find her, so we hollered again and again.

We called out her name as we went in different directions. I hollered, "Daddy, I think I heard her!" But then there was only silence, as we all became more desperate. It was nearing dusk and total darkness would soon cover the mountain. *Oh, Lord, have mercy on us!*

More than half an hour we searched, and panic had begun to set in. Just then a truck drove up with a load of coal. The driver got out, saw our fear, and for some reason walked straight over to a deep water hole under the willows. The baby, nearly concealed, hung over a half-submerged limb, drowned. We had seen the white of her bloomers, floating on the surface, thinking it was the foam that always gathered under the willows and so we kept looking. We saw right where she waded in, we could still see her little footprints. He pulled her out and, oh, God, my step-mother. . . .

Hala's screams echoed over the mountains as death closed in around us. When the man handed that little form into her mother's arms, it sounded the way the Bible describes Rachel weeping for her children, and would not be comforted. We all wailed and cried, but Hala's grief was so deep the rest of us ran away, stood afar off, and listened. My daddy went behind the smokehouse. We left Hala alone.

She rocked to and fro, holding her baby with her blonde hair streaming water over Hala's arms. Such groaning, wailing, and grief rising up into those hills and echoing back. We could not stand it. The undertaker came and took the baby, and later said only about two spoonfuls of water were found in her little lungs.

Of course we had no money to bury Shirley Ruth, but the undertaker was good and trusted Daddy to pay him later. We took her little casket back to Clay County where Mammy was buried, waded the Redbird River, and laid her at the foot of Pappy's plot. Daddy squatted there on one foot, grief too deep for tears, holding his hat in his hand—the mountain man's sign of respect—as he knelt before the rock they had set there as her little tombstone.

Our grief was awful, our sorrow terrible. It reminded me of what our grandfather, Pappy, told one day when he came home from Aunt Myrtle's restaurant in Pineville. There had been a shootout in town that day, resulting in a man's three grown sons being shot to death during some dispute. They said the boys' mother was a believer, a true saint of God, but the father wasn't saved. That day he stood over his dead boys, raising a fist toward heaven, and bitterly cursed God out loud.

Oh, to suffer that kind of grief and not know the blessed Holy Spirit, and have Him help us. Nowadays they medicate people for such deep grief so they can barely remember it. How much more healing for the

Comforter to help us bear what must be borne.

Many of those good mountain people already knew the blessed Holy Spirit, because years earlier God had sent out His Spirit across our region, and a Holy Ghost revival had set those hills on fire. My Mammy had had that experience, but the rest of us—and oh, dear God!—so many others, still walked in fear, poverty, and darkness.

Who knows what went through the minds of those parents who sent their brave mountain sons off to that great world war, boys who never had left home before in their lives, and many boys never returned to the mountains.

Always, too, you saw the mountain mothers rocking on their front porches, holding aprons up in front of weeping eyes, the day their teenage sons went to work in the coal mines. There went their boyhood forever, and all their mama's hopes, as they headed for those dark, dangerous, underground places to who knows what . . . poisonous gasses, cave-ins, or, at the least, black lung disease. How could those parents stand it, unless they had God?

Mammy knew the Comforter, but her son, our daddy, did not. You don't reach God through your mother or father, but only through a one-on-one encounter with God that our Daddy had not yet had.

Grief comes to every person on this earth at some time or other, but it seemed like it went so much deeper with those mountain people whenever they lost one of their own. They had so little anyway that such grievous loss seemed unbearable. The fear of such tragedy stalked them every day of their lives.

Fear. Like the day soon after Shirley Ruth died, a blazingly beautiful day when thousands of dry, autumn leaves dropped from the trees making such noise that my two little sisters, playing along the railroad track as they walked home from buying buttermilk from a neighbor for supper, couldn't hear the train rushing toward them.

We could see them through the window, see that old engine and caboose speeding toward them, and them dawdling on the tracks like they couldn't hear a thing. We ran outside screaming, "Get off the track! Get off the track!", even jumped up and down to get their attention, but the train rushed past and we could not see a sign of them, could only hope they had somehow saved themselves.

Then Lucy and Martha emerged from a huge drift of leaves. Lord, none of us could eat a bite of supper that night. That thing done us in. Hala said, "Lord, if I had lost them, I would have died."

Back to Straight Creek

Not long after that we were able to move back to Straight Creek, to the little house Daddy had leased out during the war. We could leave the sadness and despair of the other old place behind, could go back to a place of refreshing. We felt like it surely might bring some measure of peace to our grieving spirits.

Of course, we did not expect life to be easy there or anywhere else, and it wasn't. But for me, there would soon come a blessing far beyond anything I could ask or even think. I would encounter the

living God, in all His power. Then I could exchange
the ashes of grief for the oil of gladness.[1] I could
move out of my darkness and into His glorious light.[2]

Endnotes
1. See Isaiah 61:3.
2. See 1 Peter 2:9.

God's Got Everything Under Control

I read in the paper another earthquake tore the land
And famine is out of control.
There's fighting and dying and there's sin on every hand
And where it ends, the minds of men just don't know.

Now your valley may be dark,
And your mountains oh so high.
And you've come to the end of your road,
Just look up to Jesus, He's standing close by,
He's got everything under control.

CHORUS:

But God's got everything under control.
He's still God, and He's in charge of His own;
I can sleep like a baby, I've got peace in my soul,
God's got everything under control.
　　　　　　　　　　　—BETTY JEAN ROBINSON

4

God's Got Everything Under Control

At Christmastime in the mountains we didn't get anything. Nobody else did, so it was nothing. Sometimes Pappy would go into the mountains and get us a big holly tree with pretty berries, and sometimes we made paper chains to hang around the tree. We thought it was beautiful.

Other times, on Christmas Eve they'd tell us Santa Claus was going to come. We'd nail our long brown stockings to the mantlepiece in the same room where everybody slept, three or four in each of the two beds. You could lie there and wait, watching the flickering fire, until Daddy and Hala sneaked out of bed around midnight. They'd count out every nut and piece of candy so we'd all get exactly the same. When they dropped an orange and apple into each stocking it stretched almost down to the hearth.

We'd find those wonderful stockings early the next morning, while the smell of Hala's chicken cooking made everything even more wonderful. We did enjoy a special Christmas dinner when we got to have one.

Other times, at Christmas there was little to eat. One of those bad Christmases some of my step-mother's kin, her sister and her husband and children, walked to our house from the other side of Straight Creek, hoping they could have dinner at our house.

Since none of the daddies had cars, our means of locomotion was to walk the railroad tracks, so here came Aunt Rosette, her husband Pearl, and their little ragged children, walking on the tracks. They stayed back at the tracks, wouldn't come up to the house, but sent their boy Charles up to ask, "Can we come and eat dinner?"

We didn't even plan a special dinner that year. We couldn't afford our usual chicken dinner and banana pudding; probably meant to have cornbread and pinto beans. Daddy must have felt helpless, because he couldn't stand to turn people away. I know it hurt his pride, but he went to a neighbor's house to borrow a little money so he could go to the store. Probably he feared the man might say no, but he swallowed his pride and went anyway.

We told Hala's sister's family, "Come on in," and Daddy went to buy some stuff. We cooked what he brought home and enjoyed the best dinner. When you share with someone else, there's always a blessing. That "bad" Christmas turned into a very good Christmas after all.

At the Baptist church on the hill they had a

nativity scene program each year. As the choir sang Christmas music, suddenly someone would open the curtain made of bedsheets pinned to a wire that they had strung across the altar, and there you'd see little mountain children portraying the holy family. Oh to be Mary; it was so wonderful to be chosen to be Mother Mary, to be the one nearest to Baby Jesus. Some years I was the narrator and got to read the Christmas story from the Gospel of Matthew.

There in that high-ceilinged church with its potbellied stove and us children reenacting the birthday of the Baby Jesus, how quiet and sacred it felt. The church would be full of children who came out of the hills knowing they'd receive gifts. Two big washtubs filled with small brown paperpokes, each containing an orange, an apple, nuts, and hard candies, stood either side of the doorway.

Deacon Graydon Howard, Deacon Widener, and the other good Baptist deacons seemed overjoyed to pass out those little sacks to the shy, timid, almost fearful children. The little children would leave the church and head home so excited and happy, and the deacons would be happy for them. That's the way it's supposed to be. Those were wonderful, wonderful days.

My Special Pappy

As I said, we all walked the railroad tracks. In my bare feet I could run the tracks so fast, and we'd race, one young'un on one track and another young'un on the other. Then we would stop and dig until we found a hair the color of our sweetheart's hair (it was really a horse's hair). The railroad train and that track were our lifeline. The big cars of coal that left out of there were called "black gold," the thing that supported families in those parts. I well remember walking the tracks and picking up lumps of coal in my cracked and freezing little hands to take home for our family to burn.

I loved my Pappy, who often walked the railroad tracks with us. He'd take us out in the fall to gather walnuts, hickory nuts, and beechnuts. Sometimes he'd pick up a nut and say, "I believe this is the biggest hickory nut I've ever seen," and we'd crowd around and look, impressed, because if Pappy said it, it must be so.

Other times he'd point out the "tallest" or "prettiest" tree he'd seen since childhood, and we'd stare at this special tree and feel so lucky to see it. Pappy taught us about the beauty of the world and the goodness in it. He took time with us children and watched over us. He told some of the most wonderful stories you ever heard.

He understood animals, seemed to sense their needs, and could make sick animals well. With no formal training, Pappy was able to doctor them with liniment, stitch up their cuts, even perform surgery in an emergency. The stock would get well. Pappy was a brilliant man, a wise man, an excellent counselor.

We loved to gather around and watch Pappy take warts off the children's hands. My little sister Martha Belle, had a heart for the little dirty, neglected children in our area, and sometimes she'd bring them in and bathe them and dress them in her own clean clothes, then take them to Pappy so he could take their warts off.

Pappy would close his eyes, and we could see his mouth move a little as he rubbed those warts. We kids crowded close, trying to hear what he was saying so we could do the same thing.

We never discovered what Pappy said, but those warts always left when he rubbed them. Good old Baptist Pappy probably was praying, I believe.

Pappy taught us many wonderful things. We could smell the wind and rain before it came. He planted his crops according to the signs of the moon, and they prospered. He taught us to identify trees, rocks, animals, seasons, and made us aware of every beautiful thing God made in those mountains.

I got to where I'd draw pictures on scrap paper, on the clean side of paper my classmates threw away. Lots of times I drew pictures of pretty girls wearing pretty clothes, the way I wished I could be. One particular time, though, I drew a deer coming down to our creek to drink that good, cold water. The picture came from my imagination, a lovely deer bending to drink from our creek, with all the ferns and flowers around her. I was so proud when they put my drawing in the school superintendent's office at the county seat in Pineville.

So we traveled the railroad tracks, climbed the mountain, and scrambled over the creek banks, always finding something new and wonderful. Sometimes we went scavenging along the creek, looking for things that washed up there during previous floods.

That's where I found pieces of broken dishes for my pretend kitchen, or muddy pillowcases I could take home to wash, starch, and use. Another time we found some rings that had washed out of a faraway coal-mine commissary.

We went looking, because we had nothing. We'd pull bed sheets out of trees and wash them, starch them, and put them on our beds, all pretty and white and clean . . . treasures.

To a child, finding buried treasures means excitement. You didn't think about where it came from, you just rejoiced to dig up a bit of flowered saucer or some little knick-knack you could take home.

Springtime Floods

Floods happened regularly. If you lived in the mountains, on a creek or a river, you knew to expect them. We had to live near water, of course, so we could bathe and drink and cook. We'd haul our old iron wash pot to the sandy bank of Redbird River, prop it up on rocks, build a good fire under it and heat that pure, clean water. We'd boil our clothes with homemade lye soap. At school, two girls went to the blowing springs high up in the mountains at lunchtime and brought back a big pail of cold water, suspended over a broomstick for the children in our classroom to drink.

Flash floods came crashing off the mountain top, swelling our rivers, creeks, and streams, sometimes it came so fast it flooded your house. We kept a vigilant watch for flooding. Sometimes while Daddy was working up North, Pappy and I would sit by the fire at night and watch out for the creek to rise. At times a heavy rain would back up from Pineville, to Straight Creek from the Cumberland River.

We'd stay up all night, taking turns watching. Pappy would put a stake at water's edge to see how fast it was rising. He'd come in the house to wait, sitting by the fireplace with his cane leaning up against his chair. I'd sit beside him on a tiny cane-bottom chair, so weary I'd lean my head against his knee and doze. Pappy would check his stake at intervals. If the water was rising fast and looked like it would reach the house, we'd make a decision about when to throw the beds up against the walls and hoist the mattresses as high as we could get them.

That house was beautiful, I thought, when we cleaned it up with fresh starched sheets and shoved the canned goods up under the beds to stay cool. There was a time when walls were papered with newspapers, and when I woke up in the morning I could look at my favorite funny papers plastered up near my bed and read them for the thousandth time.

A table between the beds held a little battery radio with a ground wire leading outside and a big old Philco battery behind it. As long as that battery was good, we could get the Midday Merry Go 'Round that came out of Knoxville: Daddy wouldn't allow anything but bluegrass—Bill Monroe and the Blue Grass Boys. Sometimes we got the Grand Old Opry on Saturday nights. . . . Red Foley or Roy Acuff singing "Wreck on the Highway" or "Great Speckled Bird." Oh yes, then we would have a connection with the outside.

But this pretty house of ours—its two rooms, kitchen, and front porch made of old barn wood—had its share of floods. You could count them by the marks on the wall. We could point to a stain and say, "This was the 1940 flood," or "This one's 1945," or whatever, according to how high the water rose on a particular year.

Then came the best spring, when things were going good for us. Daddy bought a little bit of bottom land on the creek bank, where the good land is. He had the prettiest corn that June, about shoulder high and waving in the breeze. My little sister and I had each been given a calf; Daddy let on like they were ours so we'd take care of them until time to sell them. We had a big bunch of frying chickens growing, little diddlers coming on, and Irish potato blooms were hanging on the plants in that rich soil.

We loved hoeing the garden out, those rows of onions, sweet potatoes, the beds of mustard greens, lettuce, and tomato vines. We prided ourselves on all that beauty, even to the watermelon vines coming along unusually early.

One morning before daylight we wakened to hear heavy rain pounding on the tin roof, with thunder and lightening splitting the skies. At the crack of daylight Mitchell Patterson raced down the railroad track, calling out, "You'ns better git out. A flood's a'comin' at the head of this creek!"

Already things were washing out. Before we knew it, water swirled everywhere. The cows went crazy. We tried to save them and the old mule, who refused to be led. The water drowned the chickens. As we threw our beds against the wall Daddy opened windows so the water would go through and not overturn our house. He opened doors so the water could run through and the pressure not destroy it.

This was a flash flood, a danger, with rushing, mighty waters roaring off those mountains, in and out of those hollows. At daylight, we had to leave . . . had to get out fast.

Daddy let me take fifteen little diddlers I'd hatched. I put them in an old suitcase and we got out of there. Our fields were overflowing, the corn going under. We headed up the hill to Brother and Sister Lankford's house on the slate dump above all that water. Three days later I remembered that suitcase. When I opened it the poor little diddlers were staggering from a lack of oxygen, but they were still alive.

Lord, what a time! That water raged, houses came down, hitting big trees in our fields, then crashing to bits, furniture flying high. We watched one little wooden house after another get smashed into pieces with everything in it. We stood helplessly on that hill, watching the destruction, praying our house would not turn over and be lost. Dog houses, chicken houses, and every kind of animal floated past us, all desperately seeking safety.

The next day the waters began to recede. We walked down that railroad track, afraid to go home. My little sister and I looked all around at what had washed up . . . even stoves and refrigerators. People were digging other people's possessions out of the wreckage and taking them home. Anyhow, nobody knew who owned what out of all that mess.

As we walked we saw them haul a refrigerator away only to discover the body of a sixteen-year-old girl submerged beneath it. She had washed away when her house went under. That was an awful, awful time.

Daddy put on his gum boots and walked in that knee-deep mud that covered the floors of our house. His head hung down, he was so discouraged, as he began to shovel mud out of the house and that lean-to kitchen. The stove was still there, rusty and filthy, but it could be shined up with a meat skin and put back into use.

But the fields were bare, our chickens drowned, our crops destroyed, even the topsoil washed away. These are the things we cannot control, things that only God can control.

"Betty Jean. . . ."

My daddy had known more than his share of set-backs, but he still did not know the God who controls the universe. None of us did. Yet I couldn't help remembering the day I went alone to the creek bank to dig for something pretty, hoping to find something exciting.

That day, alone in the stillness and quiet, Someone spoke my name: "Betty Jean."

I looked all around, but no one was there. Then I heard it again . . . a quiet but commanding voice. "Betty Jean." Alert now, I searched for the One who was calling me, but did not see anyone else at all, so I went on digging and seeking.

Jesus, Lord of My Life

CHORUS:
Jesus, You're Lord of my life,
There're no other gods before You;
You're changing me daily from glory to glory,
Jesus, You're Lord of my life.

VERSE 1:
What did I ever do
To deserve being loved by You?
No gift in my hand did I bring,
No sweet word, no song could I sing

RECITATION:
And yet, Lord, You said I love You, because You
first loved me. I was like a little bird, caught
in a snare. I beat my wings against the thorns and
the thistles that surrounded me and I was helpless.
With wings broken and bruised, I waited silently for
my Lord to come and deliver me. My Lord did come, and
with His mighty hand, He crushed the snare that had
me bound, and He set me free.
                    —BETTY JEAN ROBINSON, ASCAP

5

Jesus, Lord of My Life

One night at the age of twelve, I had a dream. In my dream, I was walking along a long railroad track that lay ahead. I knew I had a great decision to make. Around the curve I could see a bright light streaming from Sister Lankford's house, and on the other side I saw a dark house where a mean, perverted old man lived. We children always ran from him.

I knew I must choose between the dark side of the track and the side where light and warmth shown out—Brother and Sister Lankford's little cottage.

The decision seemed important. I thought for a moment, then stepped to the side where the beautiful light was shining. Oh, how happy I felt—purely happy, like that day under the Wahoo bushes when Someone called my name. It was so sweet. . . .

What a wonderful dream for a twelve-year-old girl, one who at thirteen would be called to make that same decision—darkness or light, the most important decision we ever make.

My Most Important Decision

IT CAME ABOUT in the most ordinary sort of way. We girls had taken to playing on Mrs. Rice's porch outside her big two-story house. Nobody else had a house that big, with a wrap-around porch where children were welcome to play. Sister Rice was so sweet, a good neighbor who let us come there on rainy days, with the big drops of spring rain falling. We would sit in the porch swing, swing real high, and sing as the beautiful rain touched all of God's nature and perfumed the air with the scent of ferns.

One day some ladies we didn't know arrived, and sounds of singing soon came through those old doors. At night people were meeting to pray in Mrs. Rice's house, where every room had a fireplace, and she had linoleum rugs on her floor, and a real dining room suite. . . . Sister Rice in her long white apron and her sweet face.

People began to stop at Sister Rice's house whenever those women came. Other neighbors began to come, and they moved the beds over so they could sit on the sides of them, and lined up straight chairs near the fireplace. They set an old cane-bottom chair like my Pappy used to make, right before the fireplace that was closed for the summer. That chair was the altar. That's where you came to find Jesus, to let

Him wash your sins away.

One night I went down there. I walked down the railroad track barefooted that summer evening. I was sitting in that room with men of God crowding in, when God began to move. Sister Rice got saved, her daughters got saved, and neighbors were getting saved. That's where Sister Lankford got saved.

The men of God were preaching, and things began happening. Revival was breaking out. There was no electricity and no telephone, just lamps on Sister Rice's mantel, old coal-oil lamps flickering, casting their shadows against the ancient black-and-white pictures of ancestors hanging on the wall.

The old embroidered mantel scarves, the clean, shining lamps . . . and the flicker of that light as the preacher preached the gospel. I saw that old cane-bottom chair and knew I must go there. The Holy Ghost fire, the burning presence of God, the convicting power of God, fell over me like a hood so I could see nothing else, burning my flesh and myself away, only allowing me to see my need for my Savior.

Though I was only thirteen, I needed a Savior as much as those coal miners and those older people. I was young, but God's Word says "all have sinned, and come short of the glory of God; . . . and the Lord hath laid on him the iniquity of us all."[1]

I needed Jesus. All I remember now is that I was drawn to the altar, and I fell down before Him, fell down heavily on my scarred-up, dirty knees, weeping before the Lord who is the Spirit of conviction. I felt the spirit of repentance as I confessed and cried out to God.

Oh, they were all shouting. When I came to myself, they said I had shouted too. The room was filled with those who had found the Lord and were shouting His praises and thanking Him for saving them.

Now you know, my upbringing caused me always to be shy. Mountain children tended to be shy, maybe because we were poor, or because life was harsh, but we were timid.

That night they told me, "Honey, you shouted all over this room." I was caught up in the glory of the Lord, caught up in His presence. Shouting that He had saved my soul, that His precious sweet hands, His nail-scarred hands had touched me, and His blood had washed my sins away. I shouted and shouted. I had gone down that railroad track so poor, ragged, and barefooted, but came back up that track to my house that night as a child of the King, knowing that everything my Father owned was mine.[2]

Revival in the Hills

Everything! I was an heir and a joint heir with Jesus, my Savior. So many were saved on that side of the mountain. The Holy Ghost just flew—that precious dove just flew house to house, pleading, "Come, hear the gospel!" Many answered God's call, young people and those already old, in their forties and fifties.

Then came Sunday, the day we were to be baptized. Seems like today, you just confess, but don't change. In the Holiness way we learned in the mountains, you got saved, then baptized, sanctified, filled with the Holy Ghost, and then walked upright before Him and shared what He had done for you.

It was natural that the next step was to be baptized. We began to gather one Sunday and walked the railroad track, those saints who had been saved. The sun was shining brightly as we walked to the old railroad bridge pier that stuck up out of the cold water.

I walked barefooted. All of us were very quiet as we walked down, spreading the leaves and weeds and pushing the branches apart as we made our way down the bank and into the icy water. We stood at the edge of Straight Creek waiting for the preacher. Always there'd be two preachers with their white shirt sleeves rolled up, their shirts buttoned to the top, no necktie, but dressed in the suits they wore to preach in.

We pinned our dresses between our legs so they would stay down in the water. People who heard there'd be a baptizing, sinners and Baptists alike, gathered on the other side of the water to watch. Mamas warned their little boys not to skip rocks across the creek, not to muddy the water.

But I was with the Holiness folks on the other side of the water, the ones who believed in being saved, sanctified, baptized, and filled with the blessed Holy Ghost with the evidence of speaking in tongues.

We held hand by hand and waded into the water, which was very cold although it was summertime. That was my second wonderful experience. There is another joy that comes, one like that of being saved, when you become baptized. As the preacher lifted his hand toward heaven he brought us down into the water, then back up. Oh the joy of being plunged beneath that water, then coming up shouting and full of praise.

Everyone shouted and praised God in the water, glorifying His precious name. We held hands as we were led back out with our wet clothes and hair clinging to us, back up the bank to wrap ourselves in an old shirt or towel as we all went back up the railroad tracks.

Praising Him All Day Long

I went home and started living for the Lord. All the sadness and heaviness in my life had been lifted, all the poverty, pain, and hurt. All the rejection I had felt as a child now was hidden away in Jesus. When I dug taters I whispered His name and praised Him. When I carried water I blessed His name, just as all the old saints had told us to carry His praise on our lips all day long.[3]

I could hear Sister Lankford and the other saints as they hung their washing on the line, singing the praises of God. Voices carried across the mountain, carried for miles. They'd sing as they worked: *"He is mine, He is mine."* Or they'd sing, *"Joy in my soul, peace in my mind; Jesus, I know He is mine. He saved me when I was lost, He sanctified my soul. He filled me with the Holy Ghost, He is mine."*

At any hour of day or night some of us would gather on the side of the mountain for prayer and worship. Brother Lankford would come and lead us, coming down out of the mines about ten o'clock in the morning. We met at one house or the other, but I especially remember meeting at Brother Lankford's house on the slate dump.

Brother Lankford had been a Baptist. Sister Lankford had just gotten saved with us. Brother Lankford had been healed once as he worked in the cornfield, and he remembered that experience. After Sister Lankford got saved, he began seeking the Holy Ghost. He knew God was moving in a mighty way. Brother Lankford fought the Holy Ghost a little, but the love of God that he saw in his wife won him over. When he sought the Lord, God filled him with the blessed Holy Ghost.

A childhood picture of Brother Lankford showed him sitting on the porch with his clean overalls and white shirt, studying the Bible. He studied and read the Bible, reading every minute he wasn't in the coal mines.

We'd meet at Sister Lankford's house around ten o'clock in the morning and again at five in the afternoon. We'd gather in that little old living room with its stove, linoleum rug with the holes in it, mohair couch, and kitchen table where the fried pies were made.

We started out with singing! *"When Jacob the pilgrim was weary one day, at night on a stone for a pillow did lay; he saw in a vision a ladder so high, the bottom was on earth and the top did reach the sky. Oh hallelujah to Jesus, who died on the tree. He raised up this ladder of mercy for me. Press onward, press upward, your prize is in view. A crown of bright glory is waiting for you."*

Then we'd sing "He is mine," a good one that brings you into the Spirit, bringing us closer to Him where the blessing would fall upon everyone in the room. Then we testified, each person standing to tell what the Lord had done. The Word of God says, "They overcame him by the blood of the Lamb, and the word of their testimony" (Rev. 12:11).

Those days nothing meant anything to us except living for Him. When we left on Sunday nights after the preaching, praying, shouting, and healing, I'd fall asleep praising His name and wake up with my first words being, "Praise His holy name."

You praised God all day long, not silently but aloud. If you lived in a house with sinners, you went into the back bedroom as the Spirit directed you, and you prayed out loud. Men prayed aloud as they worked. Back and forth across our mountains you could hear prayers rising up. When Sister Rice's grandson Danny was seeking the Holy Ghost, he prayed up in his Granny's orchard—oh, how wonderful and how fearful to hear a man getting in touch with God—and a woman clear across the creek heard Danny praying.

She had no idea who it was, just heard this awesome voice crying out to get hold of God, so she fell to her knees and asked God to save her soul. She thought she heard the Lord calling forth from that mountain. Maybe she did.

Oh Lord, when the Holy Spirit moves, when that wind blows and moves, men lay down their shovels, picks, and hoes, and run to where He is gathering His people. Sometimes in the living room of that house the Spirit of God would come upon us, and we would dance in the Spirit as everyone worshiped Him.

There would be six or eight or ten of us, filling the room with our praises. No one taught us how to worship, but Jesus led us. He taught us how to pray, how to praise, how to worship. He showed us great and mighty things.

Many times I walked barefoot—no, I ran!—up that railroad track to the Lankfords' house, just as in my dream. There in my memory, warmth, light, and glory still shine out, glorious as in my heavenly vision.

Hallelujah be to God!

Endnotes

1. See Romans 3:23; Isaiah 53:6.
2. See Galatians 4:1–7.
3. See Psalm 35:28.

The Shepherd of My Valley

What would I do without Jesus, the Shepherd of my valley?
Lord, I just couldn't walk my road alone
When I'm hungry He feeds me, when I'm thirsty He's my water.
I couldn't make it without Jesus. What would I do?

CHORUS:

For when I need someone to talk to, He's always there to listen.
And when arms fold without me, He rocks me in His bosom.
What would I do without Jesus, the Shepherd of my valley?
I couldn't make it without Jesus. What would I do?

RECITATION:

When my tears flow like a river,
And when my burden gets as high as a mountain,
When the ones I have counted on have let me down,
You know they will sometimes,
You know that's when I go to Jesus.
Thank God, He's someone you can always count on.
I couldn't make it without my Jesus.
What would I do?

REPEAT CHORUS

—BETTY JEAN ROBINSON, BMI

6

The Shepherd of My Valley

We newly baptized believers had no denomination. We just knew Pentecost and believed in holiness. That is all we knew, to walk in Holiness, to act right, and even to dress right, as they taught us.

Sometimes people turn such things as what we eat and how we dress into doctrine, which, if we're not careful, can move us away from Jesus. That's the way it was with me when Hala decided to have permanents put in us girls' hair. My stepmother wasn't a Christian, remember, so right soon after I got saved Hala sold her roasting ears, took us to town, and got us permanents.

Curls and Condemnation

You see, I thought it was wrong to get your hair curled. I thought I had committed the worst sin, so I decided there was no use in my going back to church. There was no one at home who could teach me anything about holiness, so I was all alone in my decision.

The saints of God would walk down the railroad tracks on their way to prayer meeting and call me. "Honey, come on and go with us. Are you going to prayer meeting tonight?" Meanwhile, there were so many things I'd have to do if I was to go out. I'd have to set my little brother's and sister's feet in the wash pan and wash the dust off before they went to bed, and the whole time I was doing that I'd be receiving further orders.

I knew these things were the enemy's way of keeping me from church, but when I got my hair curled I thought I truly had sinned against God. I had to be obedient to my stepmother, but I still felt like a sinner.

Every time Sister Lankford and Sister Linchy Mink and the other saints passed my house and called me to prayer meeting I'd say, "I guess not. Not tonight." They didn't know how much I longed to go, and how wretched I felt over believing I had backslid.

The devil does that with every new believer— makes them feel ashamed and unworthy, like there's no use. One day I could stand it no longer. I thought, *I'm a backslidden child and have gone back on the Lord, but I'm going to go back on down there anyway.*

The Shepherd of My Valley

I'll never forget it. When I went into church I tried to hide myself from the Lord, feeling such shame, but the saints didn't even seem to notice. They didn't know anything was wrong, didn't even look at my curly hair. They didn't see how much condemnation the devil had placed on me to make me not want to serve and praise the Lord.

When we started singing that night at Mrs. Rice's house I forgot all about my hair, and the devil's condemnation had to flee. I praised the Lord and shouted, and He blessed me. He just opened the windows of heaven, and poured His blessed sweet presence on me.

You see, condemnation comes from the devil. Conviction comes from God. The Lord will gently guide us when we know we have not walked according to His Word, or when we say or think something unworthy. The Lord will let that sweet Holy Ghost conviction come upon us. I'm afraid so many of His children feel bound under a condemnation that comes straight from the devil. It pulls them down and makes them afraid to go straight to Him. Satan constantly accuses the brethren, but Jesus brings only sweet conviction. He says, "This is the way. Walk ye in it."

Those were tumultuous times, with God pulling me one way and Satan the other. I felt so alone in my home, with no one else to talk to about the things of God, and with so much harsh treatment from life. We were children, but we had adult responsibilities thrust upon us very early, because mountain life is beautiful, but it is also hard.

Alone on the Slate Dump

I'd go up on the slate dump to think—a big, big, big hill of beautiful red slate where I could sit and look out over Straight Creek. I could smell people's dinners, would know who was cooking what in our little village. It felt so peaceful, looking out over our neighbors, across the little Baptist church with its beautiful steeple, nestled there in the hills.

Indian summer, with its misty air and the smell of falling leaves. They seemed almost like tea when they got wet, like tea brewing. Oh, to let my feet wade through those leaves, to kick through them, allowing my whole being to soak in God's perfect order. That's the Indian in me, I guess. I loved God's world, His nature, then—and I still do. I don't worship what He has created, but I worship Him who created the very breath I breathe, who made such beauty for me to see, and gave me eyes to see it.

Back home, things were stressful and hard. There never was any time for joy. Daddy was a loyal, honest, hard-working man, but he was a brooding man. He could go into deep depressions. At times he walked in an awful cloud of gloom. He also had a very volatile temper, so you walked softly around him and didn't stir up his wrath.

My stepmother grew up very hard. She was abandoned by her father, then taken away from her mother by other people who raised her. Hala worked so hard, and passed that on to us. There almost never was any time for rest, just work all the time. She was a perfectionist, and made us clean things over and over.

The Shepherd of My Valley

Church was the only place I did get to go. I never saw a movie in my life, never went to a theater in my growing-up years. I never ate in a restaurant—except for an occasional hamburger at my uncle George Karloftis' restaurant in town—until I left home and started dating. I'd work so hard to get ahead those afternoons so I could go to church, only to see something come over Hala. She'd say, "You ain't going nowhere tonight. You ain't going to church."

I would get so depressed. I longed to go to the house of God, so I'd think, *There's only seven more days until another Sunday. I'll go then.*

I longed to leave all that stress, to find a peaceful life, so I'd escape sometimes to the slate dump so I could think my own thoughts. I was a dreamer. I looked at those mountains and the beauty that surrounded me, the waters rushing down the hollows, the trees, birds, butterflies, and the sounds of nature like the wind roaring through the mountains awesome as a freight train.

All that gave me joy. Very little joy came to me through our family life, it seemed, except for the love of my little sister Martha Belle, the one I took care of and loved so much. I'd take her little hand, and she was my security blanket.

Love Never Fails

I got to where I resented so much about life and its cruelty, resented the nagging, scolding, and constant demands. Resented the things I could not do or was not allowed to do, and just wanted to grow up, get away, and fulfill my dreams. Go somewhere where nobody put you down and made you feel like you were nothing.

Hala took good care of me, accepted her husband's child by another woman, but I was the only dark-haired child in that house. The others were blond and blue-eyed, little Scotch-Irish descendants, so with my dark hair and Indian features I felt like an outsider. Nobody's fault, but that's how I felt.

And though I did well enough at school, and mostly enjoyed school, I felt shame there as well. We took biscuits to school for lunch, a sign we were poor. My little sister and I would hide behind the big beechnut trees and eat our biscuits. And we couldn't wait for May to come so we could take off those ugly old brown stockings, those thick things that made you feel you weren't one bit pretty.

One day I went to the spring for water, and our neighbor, who was not always kind, said, "Why don't you go home and take off that ragged dress and put on a clean dress?" I wondered if she didn't know I didn't have a clean dress, that I wore my only dress all week and then my stepmother would wash it. That way we had a clean dress to wear on Sunday.

Things spoken out of turn can hurt a child so bad. We never know when we may wound someone, especially the poor, the destitute, and needy. They may already feel hopeless. It destroys something in children to mock them when they are poor.

But I was learning that Jesus says to love such people and forgive them. Jesus said to bless those who curse you and despitefully use you.[1] You can't do that in your flesh, you can't just will yourself to love, love, love people.

But God can give you that love that helps you forgive. Through Jesus, and Him only, you truly can bless those who despitefully use you and forgive each one who hurts you.

The old saints I knew taught me that love never fails. Everything else passes away, but God is love, and He is forever and amen.

To this day I can feel the love of those old saints of God I knew in the mountains. Even later, in my backslidden years, I never felt judgment, criticism or accusation from them. When they came to you they offered pure love, never condemnation. And when they'd leave, you felt like they left something with you that was so sweet and full of peace. They left Jesus with you.

In other churches I found men and women who were so cold, hard, and critical, so good at fault-finding that they made you feel you had failed the Lord. I always felt so guilty and scared around them. I draw nothing from remembering those people. They left me with nothing to feed me, nothing to remember and take away.

Today I still feed upon the love of Brother and Sister Lankford, Brother Hatfield, Sister Mink, Sister Rice, and so many of the other old saints. I still feel their love and kindness. And when I reflect upon their love, I feel filled up; they minister to me though they have been gone for so many years.

Love never fails. They have gone to be with Jesus, yet their love still ministers to me. Oh Lord, give me love. Do you know how to get that kind of love? Get Jesus. The more of Jesus I have in my life, the more love I'll have for everyone around me.

Sister Lankford loved everybody. She'd say, "Oh, honey, if I could, I would put my arms around the whole world and draw them to my bosom!" That's Jesus; He came to save the whole world, came to seek and to save that which was lost. Jesus wants to shine His love through us so that, like Sister Lankford, we can help lighten up this dark old world.

The Other Side of the River

Well, then Daddy decided he wanted to move over to the other side of the river, the other side of Straight Creek, to where there was a store and a post office. It was where we could get to the post office without falling in the creek trying to walk across icy rocks in the wintertime.

I liked the idea, since there was a store over there, and we would live close to the highway, which we called the "pike."

So Daddy moved us on over there and bought Mr. Lisenby's house, where I grew up from age fourteen until I left home. The house still sits on Straight Creek close to where the old swinging bridge used to be.

I don't know why we needed to be close to the post office, since we rarely heard from anybody. Anyhow, one of us always went to the post office early in the morning. But it was nice to live near the store where every now and then we would get a loaf of light bread.

The Shepherd of My Valley

Now we were across the creek from my Holiness friends, and I didn't get back to see them anymore. I could look across the creek, but I didn't get back there.

But their love had already taken root in my young girl's heart, and nothing could tear it out. I would go on from there, just as I eventually left the very mountains that fed my childhood, but some things you cannot ever uproot and replace in your life.

I carry the love of those sweet saints with me wherever I go, just as surely as I carry Jesus with me. Time and distance mean nothing. And just as you could not possibly take those mountains and those mountain ways out of my heart and soul, you cannot take away the lasting love of those precious saints of God.

I praise God for all He gave me through them.

Endnotes
1. See Matthew 5:44.

On the Way Home

Jesus is coming, can't you see it everywhere?
This old world's rumbling, can't you feel it in the air?
Neighbor, tell your neighbor, sing a happy song;
It's time to get started on the way home.

Listen to the message, oh, can't you hear the call?
Jesus is the key to overcome it all.
Let's tell it on the radio, and talk it on the phone;
Get everybody started on the way home.

Leaders, tell your soldiers they'd better lay their guns
    down,
Love is the victor, oh, can't you hear the sound?
For Jesus is coming from His mighty throne;
It's time to get started on the way home.

CHORUS:
On the way home, on the way home,
It's time to get started on the way home.
Preacher, talk about it, sing it in your song,
Get everybody started on the way home.

—BETTY JEAN ROBINSON

7

On the Way Home

Up on the hill from the little house beside the creek was the old Missionary Baptist Church built by the coal company. I was away from my little band of Holiness people now. I could look across the creek and see them, but I didn't get back over there. We started going up the hill to the little Baptist church with its beautiful wood pews and floors and its potbelly stove where we met such wonderful saints of God—those precious Baptist people, Sister LeFevers, Brother and Sister Graden Howard, Brother and Sister Smith, Brother and Sister Martin, and so many more.

They never preached the Way—you know, being baptized in the Holy Ghost—but they preached the cross and the blood of Jesus, and used the old hymnbooks from which I learned so many good songs. I loved those songs and learned to sing them.

Front Porch Harmonizing

My little sisters and I learned to sing from sitting on the porch harmonizing, with Daddy singing bass. Lucy Mae, Martha Belle, and I harmonized so well they soon asked us to sing at the Baptist church. We'd climb up the side of the mountain and go to church, where we'd sing some of the songs they liked—"Take Up Thy Cross and Follow Me" and others.

We had wonderful harmony, so soon they asked us to sing regularly. I was fourteen, Lucy Mae was eleven, and Martha Belle was six. Lucy Mae sang a wonderful, full alto, little Martha sang tenor, and I took the lead.

One week the church held a revival and invited Preacher W. W. Nails to speak. Preacher Nails was a bold, fiery Christian, very active on those mountains. He took a stand against whiskey in Bell County and Harlan County and received death threats for it. He had a weekly radio program in Middlesboro, Kentucky, which aired each Sunday . . . *The Shut-In Hour.*

Preacher Nails lived in Harlan County with his family. He liked the way the Rhodes Sisters sang, so he invited us to appear with him on the radio each week and to travel with him and sing at various church revivals. Early every Sunday morning Preacher Nails would pick us up and take us to station WMIK in Middlesboro, where he would preach and we would sing.

On the Way Home

Moving North With the Gospel

Now, you need to know a little about those mountains to understand Preacher Nails, and why churches like ours and men of God like him are so important to our nation. As you know, each year young men left the Kentucky coal mines and went north to work. There was a steady stream of good workers, some of our best talent, moving to Michigan, Ohio, Indiana, and other parts.

These were wonderful young people, moving so they wouldn't have to spend their lives in the coal dust where they faced possible death by cave-ins, poisonous gas, or black lung disease. Their mothers would urge them not to go near the mines, to move away where they could find work. And where these people moved, they carried their gospel with them. Some of America's strongest Pentecostal churches came out of those young Kentucky folks, products of that great move of the Holy Ghost that happened a generation before them.

They streamed up North to work, but longed to return home. Mountain people are clannish. They'd live from weekend to weekend to come back to the mountains to see their people. When they returned, the rest of us would laugh at some of them because they'd try to talk like northern folk. We'd tease them and say, "Y'all just been up there two weeks, and you already come back 'talking proper.'"

Other people's talk, speech that was different from the mountaineers' speech, we called "proper." But even if those people stayed away long enough to talk proper, they always kept a longing in their hearts for the mountain home most knew they'd never see again.

For the coal miners, life was always dangerous and often violent. When they called a strike, times were so hard for us. So many miners, like Merle Travis's son, owed their souls to the company store. They suffered. Many years later I wrote a song called "Shotgun Row" that described such times.

The Perils of Moonshine Whiskey

Preacher Nails was one of the men who became a light in that darkness, and preached salvation to the hopeless and the destitute. He preached against whiskey. This courageous Christian man took a stand. He went on the radio and asked people to vote against whiskey in a local option coming up. He became extremely controversial. Again and again his life would be threatened, and he expected to be ambushed and killed. Still, Preacher Nails was fearless. He stood his ground, and whiskey got voted down.

During all this controversy we girls were riding with him through those mountains. We'd travel at night and go around those curves where someone might be waiting with a gun aimed at the windshield of a car as we traveled to a revival in those Kentucky hills.

"Now girls," Preacher Nails would say, "if they start shooting, they only want to kill old Preacher Nails. Girls, they don't want to bother you, so if they start shooting y'all get down in the floorboard of the car and lay real quiet."

I don't know what the preacher thought, but Lucy Mae, Martha, and I felt no fear. So we traveled on, preaching, singing, and ministering, and Preacher Nails was instrumental in getting whiskey out of the region. At one time in Harlan County they talked about electing a woman sheriff because so many of the male law enforcement officers were shot and killed.

My High-School Years

Those were my high-school years. We spent our spare time singing at revivals, churches, and on the radio. But during those years Daddy never allowed me to attend a ballgame. We never did anything but go to school, work in the house and in the fields, and sing.

Every day I got up early to build the fire and get it started. Daddy would sit near the kitchen stove and drink his coffee. He "saucered" it, as we called it, pouring hot coffee into the saucer to cool, then drinking from the side of the saucer.

Sometimes I'd pack Daddy's dinner bucket with a pint jar of home-canned peaches, a jar of pinto beans, a slab of cornbread, and a jar of water. Then I'd hurry to catch the school bus that took me to Bell County High School.

Those high-school years were not happy years for me. Only my gospel singing made me happy. I longed to participate in some of the things that went along with growing up, but was not allowed. Once some classmates asked me to be a majorette, said I'd look pretty in the majorette costume. How embarrassing! I told them I didn't want to do it, but that wasn't true. I thought the other girls looked so pretty in those outfits, and I would've loved to look like them. But I knew not to even think about it, because Daddy would never allow us to wear short dresses and show off that way.

The reality was, we were poor. I had very few clothes, which I did my best to keep clean and ironed so I could look the best I could. We had a dime for lunch, which bought a pop and a bag of potato chips, and maybe an apple. A hot lunch cost twenty-five cents, which was too much for me. A hot lunch was cornbread, pinto beans, and cherry Jell-O, and it sure would have tasted good.

After school Hala had plenty of chores waiting for us; carrying in coal, fetching kindling, all kind of jobs. We had to do homework before dark so we could get to bed early. Then it was up early, return to school, just studying and work, studying and work, never getting to participate in ordinary teenage activities.

The little Baptist church took more and more of a place in my heart. The old church bell rang, bidding us to come to God's house. Whenever the church doors opened you could hear them singing "Amazing Grace," heavenly music floating across the mountain, and the beautiful old hymns faithfully ringing out from that little Southern Baptist Missionary Church to touch many a sinner and heal many a saint's bruised and hurting heart.

On the Way Home

The Class of '53

As Betty Jean Rhodes toiled and sang her way through high school, some wonderful things did happen. Being voted Prettiest Senior in the Class of '53 was an amazing surprise. I didn't consider myself the prettiest, but the idea that my classmates liked me enough to bestow that honor on me made me feel a part of my senior class.

Mr. Asher, our school principal, was a wonderful man who saw all his students as equals, and didn't look down on those from the mountains whose parents didn't have much money. He seemed eager to bring forth the mountain children's talents, to encourage them to make more of themselves.

He helped those little old boys put up a basketball hoop on the side of a barn, where the boys would secretly throw and throw the ball, practice and practice, hoping to get a break someday. Mr. Pursifull, a wonderful teacher, would urge them to become winners; he encouraged them to go after scholarships. Mountain children are highly intelligent.

In my case, he noticed the pictures I got to draw all around the gymnasium wall during my senior year, pictures of the different mascots for teams that played there during the year. Mr. Pursifull said, "You have a lot of talent. Why don't you go to art school?"

He went to the trouble of getting all the information for me, but I didn't want to go. I loved to sing. Most of all, I loved to sing my gospel songs. I didn't know what I would do with my life after high school, couldn't tell Mr. Pursifull my plans, because I had no idea. I just knew I wanted to sing.

Wanted by the FBI

One day some agents from the Federal Bureau of Investigation in Washington, D.C., went to the principal's office. Soon Mr. Asher sent for me and another girl named Fannie to come to the office. Fannie and I edged in there, a little scared, wondering what in the world was going on. They asked the two of us if we'd like to go to Washington—and work for the FBI!

That opportunity opened up out of nowhere, I thought, and I knew I must accept it. I knew I'd have to go away from home to work—there were no jobs in Bell County—and I'd not wanted to think about it. Daddy's dream for us girls was that we'd be able to get an office job. To him, that spelled success.

Daddy had worked so hard for us always, and I wanted to make him proud of me. I knew that it meant leaving my singing, leaving my gospel music, leaving the church, leaving home, and leaving the mountains I loved.

Standing there in Mr. Asher's office, all those thoughts went through my mind, and I felt terribly sad. Still, Fannie would be going too, so at least I'd have a friend with me. That was some comfort. I swallowed hard, looked up from where I had been studying my shoes, and said I'd go to Washington.

First, we had to take a civil service test, and then they investigated us thoroughly to see if our backgrounds met their requirements. Anyone had to have a good reputation to be accepted by the FBI and its director, Mr. J. Edgar Hoover. Well, I passed, and I was committed to the move. Meanwhile, Fannie had decided she wouldn't go.

"Going up North," as we called it, was supposed to be very dangerous, folks said. I'd never been North, of course, other than to Baltimore that one winter. I had never been much of anywhere, and felt quite timid about it. At the very least, I was about to leave my own culture and everything I knew behind me. The Rhodes Sisters would have to disband. And to top it all off, where I was going, I'd have to talk "proper."

Still, I wanted Daddy to be proud of me, and I had to find a job somewhere. Daddy went to the bank and borrowed three hundred dollars on his good name, money I'd pay back after I went to work for the government. Oh, that was a big step.

Alone and Apprehensive

Soon after I graduated from Bell County High School in 1953, I found myself headed for Washington, D.C. For once, I was dressed up good enough even for Uncle George's restaurant. I stopped by on my way out of town. My uncle saw me and motioned, "Come here. Honey, I am so proud of you!" he exclaimed. He handed me a five-dollar bill, this man who loved and believed in America, and said, "You go on and work for the government, and make something of yourself."

My money was pinned in my underclothes, hidden beneath the white sharkskin suit Preacher Nails and his wife gave me . . . a pretty suit, set off by my red straw hat with flowers on the brim, and my white gloves.

To comfort myself about the upcoming trip and all the unknown things that lay ahead, I thought back to the summer before. I'd worked at the laundry, ironing sheets for eleven dollars a week, pulling sheets through a steaming roller, matching the corners exactly, then folding the scalding hot cloth perfectly—all for twenty-five cents an hour.

The work was so hot and exhausting that the elderly women who had been there for years looked as if they could barely get through the day. Sometimes on our lunch hour we'd throw ourselves across a laundry cart for five minutes just to get off our feet. It was grueling work, but worth it, I thought, because I had a little money. You could buy a bologna sandwich for a dime and have a chocolate milk with it for lunch. I was able to take some of that money and buy fabric so we three sisters could have some matching dresses when we went out singing. Yes, the work was horribly hot and tiring, but so worth it. . . .

One day my boss at the laundry came in and asked me a question: "You plannin' to keep on working here?"

I told him no, I was going to quit at the end of summer and begin my senior year at high school.

"Good," he said "because if you didn't, I was going to fire you right now. This is no kind of work for a girl like you." He didn't want me to stay on, pulling those hot sheets between two huge rollers, then when I got too old to do that, stand and iron men's shirts like the poor old grannies who worked there.

However, I was used to hard work. At age nine I started cooking for field hands. We would go early to the fields while they were still wet with dew. Near dinnertime I would leave the fields and go back to the house to fix potatoes, fatback, cornbread, and open a jar of pickled beets for dinner—standing over that old hot stove hour by hour, like Hala was used to doing.

No wonder Daddy was proud that I could get an office job in Washington, D.C. If I could only get used to leaving, could swallow the lump in my throat and start believing this was a *good* thing.

Pappy's Principles

There I was, sitting in the Greyhound Bus station in Pineville, alone and apprehensive. Then I heard a familiar step and a well-beloved voice in that bus station. *Pappy Rhodes!* He moved through the rows of benches, searching for me with his eyes. He'd walked all this way to see me, wouldn't ever take a bus, always walked down the railroad track though we begged him not to come that way because with his bad hearing a train could hit him.

Here he was now, standing before the black people in that segregated bus station, bringing them some news. "I want to tell you something," he said. "They passed a law in Washington, D.C. It says you can drink out of the same water fountain over there that we can. You can sit over there with us and we can sit over here with you.

"You're as good as we are, and we're good as you are; we're all the same."

I felt scared. *Pappy, don't talk like that. Hush, Pappy,* I thought. Pappy was a just and fair-minded man, a man without prejudice, and he thought he was passing on some of the biggest and most important news he could possibly bring. He loved every person he ever met, I believe.

My sweet old Pappy had walked the railroad track all the way to the bus station in Pineville saying, "Them crazy old cars on the pike—they can kill ye!" Carrying his walking stick in case he met up with a dog, he had come all that way just to say goodbye to Betty Jean, who was leaving home. My heart filled up.

Pappy handed me a package wrapped in brown paper. "Betty Jean, child, I brought something you're going to need," he said. "Put this in your suitcase and take it with you."

That dear old loving man had brought me a washboard, a small version of the one we used in the old wash tub. I put that little bitty washboard in my cardboard suitcase on top of my clothes. I was taking a bit of my pappy with me, taking a reminder of my life at home, and I felt loved and comforted.

Pappy Rhodes stayed with me until that smelly old bus pulled into the station, and I boarded it, not knowing what my future might hold, going into a world I'd never seen before. The washboard went too. I used it, and it helped.

He Careth for Me

CHORUS 1:
He careth for me, He cares for me,
My name is written on the palm of His hand:
I can't get too far away that His eyes cannot see,
He is my Father, He careth for me.

VERSE 1:
When I cry tears, when I feel rain,
When I am lonely, when I feel pain,
His love reaches down into my heart where no man can see;
He is my Father, He careth for me.

RECITATION:
The Lord is my shepherd and I shall not want. He maketh
me to lie down in His green pastures. He leads me beside His
still waters. He restores my soul. Yea, though I walk through
the valley of the shadow of death, I will fear no evil. I will say
of the Lord, He is my refuge and my God, and in Him will I
trust.
Though a thousand shall fall at my side and ten thousand at
my right hand, it shall not come nigh me. Oh child, cast
all your cares upon Him, for He careth for you.

CHORUS 2:
He careth for you, He cares for you. Listen child,
Your name is written on the palm of His hand;
You can't get too far away that His eyes cannot see.
He is your Father, He careth for you.
Yes, He is my Father, He careth for me.

—BETTY JEAN ROBINSON

8

He Careth for Me

Maybe you're young and scared, leaving home for the first time in your life. That old bus is driving farther and farther away from your mountain home, taking you to a huge city full of strangers who don't know you and don't care a thing about you. You forget who *does* care. You forget that He is beside you on that bus, going with you into the unknown future.

Fear, the kind of fear I felt that day, can overwhelm your feelings and make you believe you're committing the biggest mistake of your life. Riding that old Greyhound bus from Pineville to Knoxville, thinking of my Pappy and all the others, I felt more and more uncertain. There was a five-hour layover in Knoxville before the bus to Washington, D.C. arrived, and during those five hours I grew steadily more terrified.

What if I missed that bus? What if I got on the *wrong* bus and went somewhere else? As my anxiety and loneliness increased everything got blown out of proportion. My fears kept me from realizing that God always, always careth for me—and you.[1]

After a long day's journey, the bus at last pulled into the Washington terminal, well after dark. I squinted at my instructions, written on a small piece of paper and clutched in my hand. I was to take a taxi to my schoolmate's sister's house, where I'd stay until reporting to work.

The cab ride went on and on, so I took a fresh scare: *Where are we going? I don't know this man. He's liable to kill me. . . .* At last we arrived, I paid the driver, and let the young woman who talked like me lead this thoroughly worn-out traveler into a nice bedroom. Thank God for the hospitality of friends.

A Whole New World

The next morning I opened my eyes and ears to see and hear everything I could soak up about our nation's capitol. What a huge, beautiful, impressive place—and how dreadfully homesick I felt, how much I longed to be back in my mountains! I had to listen extra hard to the many instructions I was given at work, so scared I would overlook something. I walked down the world's longest corridors, answered so many questions, filled out so many papers. Oh, this decision was definitely a mistake!

Soon, of course, I discovered that the other new girls felt exactly the same way. Mr. J. Edgar Hoover, our boss, was a great patriot who believed in staffing his bureau with people of the highest character. Even us ordinary workers, someone like me, had to undergo almost the same type of character investigation required of a special agent. Our boss insisted on a squeaky-clean organization. In those days, a person's character and integrity counted for a lot.

Mr. Hoover took a paternal interest in his people. Young women like me, for instance, were assigned to nearby boardinghouses, where I feel certain the owners had been well checked out. I had a room in a large house on beautiful Embassy Row, next door to the British Embassy, but though it was grander than any place I'd ever lived before, I grew violently homesick.

My two roommates and I, like other young people among the FBI personnel, came from all over the United States. Soon I got used to being teased about my accent and being asked where I was from. Since nobody seemed to know about Straight Creek, Kentucky, I'd say I was from around Cumberland Gap.

"Where's that?" they'd ask.

So I'd say, "Near Kudjo Cave." By now they'd be laughing and acting surprised, and I'd get put out with them that they'd never heard of that cave—a local tourist attraction I supposed everybody in the United States had heard of. They kidded me and laughed, teasing, and I was so innocent I never knew they were doing it.

Work kept us good and busy. They assigned me to the Identification Division as a typist. Fingerprints on big cards arrived from law departments everywhere in the United States and my job was to type information on those cards, including all information about any previous criminal record for each person. Some of the people had been arrested fifty or even one hundred times, while others were new. These cards and fingerprints would be kept on file in Washington.

It was steady, sometimes very interesting work. Today, in the computer age, it's hard to imagine all that information being collected by hand, and the long time it took to gather it and send it out. It wasn't hard work, but you were expected to do what you were assigned to do, and do it thoroughly.

Those first months seemed to stretch out forever. I couldn't seem to adapt, couldn't seem to get over my loneliness and homesickness. After a while I found I couldn't make myself eat. My weight dropped from my usual one hundred and five pounds, to just under ninety pounds. Even at my short five-foot height that looked terribly skinny.

Slowly, though, I came out of it. I discovered that the thing that helped was to stay busy. To my surprise, I became quite popular. I had lots of dates and good times, even several proposals of marriage. People told me I was pretty; sometimes I even felt pretty.

One day Johnny, the man who owned the house where I boarded, asked me to consider the local Veteran of Foreign Wars' chapter's nomination for Poppy Queen. To my surprise, they chose me, and I'll never forget the thrill and the honor of meeting Vice President Richard Nixon, a gracious man, and having my picture in the paper.

He Careth for Me

I spent several years in that beautiful, awesome city, mostly longing to leave it. I was outside my culture. I felt sad most of the time, even though I made friends easily. Some of the other girls felt the same way; they never got over their terror and homesickness.

Someone From My Hills

At work one day, another young typist asked me to come over to her desk and meet a young fellow from my part of the country. William Harold Robinson, a brilliant young man, had been assigned to fingerprint identification and worked upstairs. Harry came from Knoxville, Tennessee, just seventy-five miles south of my home, and we took to each other immediately. When he asked for a date, I accepted. Who *wouldn't* respond to Harry's charisma and beautiful smile?

By then, I tell you that the Bible Sister Lankford gave me didn't get opened very often. Daily Bible reading had been left back in Kentucky, and I had quit praying too. My new world had begun to consume all my time; somehow, I just left Jesus out. Though I had not become rebellious, I had all but forgotten about the Lord.

Life got so busy. There were new roommates, the big city, going to work every day, writing home often to tell everybody everything . . . And the regular paychecks. Oh, what a busy life I led.

Young people from other places laughed at my hillbilly accent. But they liked me, I reckon; they all gathered around. Anyhow, lots of boys wanted to date me. They didn't mind the way I talked, but wanted to date me because I was from the South.

I was a good girl who kept herself pure for her wedding day. That conviction stayed with me no matter how strong the temptation, because I had been taught that a young woman should not have that kind of relations with a young man, but with your husband only. If a young lady did yield, no decent young man would want her after that; it's how we were taught. I'm glad we had those morals back then. America's come a long way—in the wrong direction, I'm afraid. Maybe there would be fewer broken homes.

After Harry Robinson and I began to date, nobody else seemed to count. He was handsome, brilliant, charming, and from my part of the country. He had a way about him that made me feel secure . . . and I needed that.

Harry also was a young man on his way to the top. Highly skilled at fingerprint identification, he was one of the first men to be chosen for training in a new and highly technical field—computers, with all their complex mystery to us ordinary people.

With that fast track up the governmental ladder, Harry's high-strung temperament began to increase. He worked hard and got stressed out often. As we drew ever closer to marriage, some of our friends noticed, and tried to warn me. "Betty Jean, I saw him push you and get angry with you over nothing."

Yes, he did that, but then he'd apologize and talk to me, and I'd somehow end up believing it must have been my fault, so I'd apologize to him. Anyhow, the poor man worked so hard, always working at that old highly technical stuff. . . .

Wedding Bells and More Stress

We married there in Washington, D.C., in a Methodist church I found, because neither of us went to church or had a church home at that time. But I did believe you should be married in church.

Harry was an excellent provider and what most women would consider a wonderful catch. However, he was always on edge, and I had to tiptoe around him. His temper would lash out when I least expected it and, as his friends had warned me, he could turn mean.

Marriage added to his stress, I believe. Harry's father had abandoned him and his mother when he was a small boy and all his life his mother had emphasized that he must take full responsibility as head of the house when he got married. I believe Harry felt the full weight of that responsibility. He certainly worked hard to provide, bought nice houses, and used his money prudently, upgrading each house so he could sell it and buy the next one. But all that responsibility, something so familiar to him and to me, all that work and no release from the mounting stress, well . . . he became so volatile that I often felt afraid of my husband.

Our daughter Rebecca, our firstborn, was born in a Catholic hospital in Washington. For more than twenty hours I was there alone, afraid, experiencing labor pains and feeling so afraid. Harry went home and played gin rummy with his friends while he waited, and I guess I thought that was normal, the way it should be.

At one point I looked up and saw a nun looking down into my face. I remembered I had written "Protestant" on my entry form, so I wondered . . .but the nuns and the Mother Superior would come to me from time to time, and treated me so very kindly.

At last a little foreign doctor came, held my hand, and told me not to be afraid; that everything would be all right. "You're not alone," he said, "I'm right here." He showed such compassion for me.

God knew where I was and sent that doctor and the nuns to help me, to comfort and assist me. I guess my husband, who had not had a father himself, had no idea that he should share Becky's birth with his wife.

After Rebecca's birth I returned to my job, working the night shift, dealing with some weakness and other health problems and learning how to take care of my wonderful baby. It was a sad, sad time, because I had begun to realize how alone and unwanted I really was. Then some physical complications set in, causing infection and terrible weakness. I had to go back to the hospital for surgery.

By now, totally exhausted, it was obvious to everybody that I'd have to resign my job. I hated that, because Mr. Hoover and everyone else had been good to me. Mr. Hoover took a personal interest in his employees, and we all worked very well together. The letter of resignation I wrote marked the end of an important chapter in my early life.

Young men in government had a strong chance of

being selected to become part of the incoming computer age, and Harry Robinson was right out in front. Sometimes he stayed at the office day and night. That was especially true when he was working one case I remember, that of a kidnaped executive. Harry and his coworkers had to record the serial numbers from all the ransom money.

A Move to Nashville

By now, major corporations had begun to seek these government-trained, computer-educated men, and Harry and I wanted to come South. When he got an offer from a major Nashville, Tennessee, corporation, he decided to take it. Nashville is just five hours away from the mountains where I grew up, and I would be so glad to see my folks again. Life had become so lonely, so empty, for me, and I had become so afraid of Harry's increasing acts of violence, that I dared to hope things might change for the better. I took my little girl Rebecca, and we moved to Nashville to join her father who had gone on ahead.

So many young women like me sense they are making a mistake, yet something drives them on. They marry someone they already are afraid of, because they don't know what else to do. By the time I married, of course I was a thorough backslider, someone who had once known God, yet departed from Him.

I never went to church. The closest I came to going to church during those years was the time before I was married, when I peeped inside the door of the huge Cathedral of St. John in Washington. It was almost an overpowering sight. I guess I was looking for the little potbelly stove, the deacons, and the shouting, singing, and praising. That's all I knew growing up; to me, that was God. The Lord was not to be found in that great cathedral. So I tiptoed out, quiet as a mouse.

I didn't commit big sins, but you don't have to commit big sins to grow cold in the Lord. You just leave Him out of your life. Day after day you forget Him, and pretty soon you are backslidden in heart. He's still there, but He is no longer part of your life.

I was away from God, living in spiritual adultery, loving the world more than I loved Jesus, living for my marriage and whatever else happened to come along, living with the violence that had become a regular part of my life. Dreams all gone, hopes beginning to fade.

Maybe something good could happen in Nashville, I thought. I'd never been there. All I knew about the place was what I heard on that battery radio back home, when we listened to the Grand Old Opry that was broadcast out of there every Saturday night.

What else did they have in Nashville? Lord, I didn't know. But the corporation that hired Harry paid to move us, so Harry and Rebecca and I struck out for Nashville, Tennessee.

Endnotes
1. See 1 Peter 5:7.

He Made Me to Sing a New Song

VERSE 1:
The first song I wrote was a sad song,
A song filled with loneliness;
Then I wrote a song even sadder,
They sang it from the East Coast to the West.
And wherever lonely men gathered,
The juke box would play them my song;
Broken women betrayed and forsaken
Would listen and cry all alone.

VERSE 2:
Then I made it big down in Nashville,
Penned a number-one song to my name.
They passed out sweet congratulations,
Bestowed on me honor and fame.
But like Judas, I threw down their money,
And the fame only left me more alone;
Then I cried out, "Dear Jesus, please help me,"
And He gave me a beautiful song.

CHORUS:
He made me to sing a new song, yes He did,
He forgot I had ever done wrong;
He gave me love this old world could never give to me,
When He made me to sing a new song.

VERSE 3:
Now I write all my songs about Jesus,
Lift men's hearts from the bottle to the sky;
I tell lonely women that Jesus loves them,
And He'll wipe the teardrops from their eyes.
I've come too far now, and time's too precious,
To ever go down that road where I have been;
I've got a new song in my heart and I'm gonna sing it,
And tell the world Christ is coming again.

—BETTY JEAN ROBINSON

9

He Made Me to Sing a New Song

For Harry, Nashville meant hard work, success, and moving right up the corporate ladder. He had the brains and the skills, and business leaders scrambled to find computer programmers like my husband, competing with the other big businesses to see which could change over to computers the fastest. Harry had a succession of high-powered jobs in banking, mortgage companies, and others, always challenging himself more, learning more, succeeding more, and probably earning more than most other young men his age.

My life consisted of tending to the house we bought, and caring for my beautiful blonde, green-eyed Rebecca, who looked so much like her father. Soon a second daughter, Elizabeth Kimberly, dark-haired and dark-eyed like me, joined our family.

Now there were two little girls, and a wife who was afraid of her husband.

Harry always provided for our material needs exceptionally well; we had beautiful clothes and several beautiful homes, each just a little nicer than the one before. But all this came with a heavy price tag. Ugly scenes, unhappiness, criticism, and discord ruled our home. Harry's childhood unhappiness never got resolved, but seemed to fester and finally spill over on all the rest of us. Since he never felt peace, neither could we.

On the Way to the Top

So often as men become successful their jobs become Number One. They're on the thrones of their lives. A wife or children had better not get in the way, because that man is on the way to the top, working so hard to make a good living. "I'm just trying to make things better for you," Harry would say. "I'm keeping you in a beautiful home, aren't I?"

I wasn't used to a beautiful home. *Just give me a one-room shack and peace,* I'd think, but I wouldn't dare say something like that aloud. Peace is wonderful; I longed for it, but I still didn't realize that one reason I didn't have it was because I was a backslider.

Not only had I left God, the church, and everything I knew as truth, but by now I had come to realize my husband actually did not believe in God. He held many New Age views; each man's personal powers and development represented all there is of

God, in Harry's opinion. He believed our lives and futures were entirely up to us. "God helps those who help themselves," he'd say.

You can decide to marry a man or woman then later learn that person's beliefs deny totally everything you know as true. I couldn't mention the name Jesus; it made him furious. He believed man descended from apes. I was far away from my roots, and married to someone whose beliefs were so contrary to my own.

Even as a backslidden Christian, I viewed the world through spiritual eyes. But my husband and I were so incompatible that I dared not verbally give God the credit for any of our good blessings. Harry's hard work, not God's goodness, was responsible for all our good fortune, according to him.

Loneliness Births a Song

As we grew apart, deep loneliness entered my life. Even with our two darling little girls, I felt lonelier, more unhappy, than I ever had in childhood. We did very little together as a family. A hard-working man deserves to go off fishing with his friends all weekend, Harry believed, so he'd curse me and leave.

As time passed and the little girls grew, somewhere a song began in my heart; not a song about Jesus, but a song about loneliness. Years earlier, back when we Rhodes Sisters sang on the radio, I wrote my first song. It was about the cross and the blood of Jesus. I wrote it in the old songbook we used to sing from on Preacher Nails' radio program, *The Shut-In*

Hour, back when we sang in Middlesboro, Kentucky. Today, as a professional songwriter, I know that first little song was laid out very well. It was written well enough that I could sing it today, and when I read those words now it makes me know that as a young girl I fully understood that my Savior paid an enormous price to save my soul.

I Know My Savior Suffered

On Calvary I see such suffering,
Such heartaches there never was known;
Like a lamb He was led to the slaughter,
And praise Him, He died there alone.

CHORUS:
Oh how He suffered, it hurts me so much to say;
But oh, how He saved me. His love I could never repay.

Oh brother, do you love Him?
Are you ashamed of His grace?
Are you willing to suffer for Jesus,
And repay Him for taking your place?

That's why for Him I will suffer,
For Him I will bear scorn and shame;
It will all be worthwhile in Heaven,
To sing there and praise His sweet name.

Before I lived out the prophecy I had written in verse three of my first song, my second song, and the ones that followed, seemed destined to bring me worldly fame, Nashville-style, rather than to cause me to suffer for Jesus. The fact was, those Nashville songs, written from a heart burdened with sadness and personal despair, were written only to ease my heart and release some of its sadness and feelings of hopelessness. By pure chance, they seemed to touch others who felt the same way.

A Ring for a Guitar

For some reason, about that time Harry sold my engagement ring and bought me a guitar. I can't quite figure out why he sold my ring to do it, because we had plenty of money, but anyhow he did, without consulting me.

I had never played an instrument, though they told me my birth mother, Annie Gray, played the guitar. I remember my daddy playing the banjo. My family members could all sing good; my mother and daddy both sang very well, and my stepmother, Hala, also sang pretty. I grew up hearing the sounds of good voices and good instruments; to me, music is a big part of natural life.

I bought an instruction book for a dollar that taught me how to play chords on the guitar. The moment I first put my fingers on that D-chord, I heard melodies in my head. That music I heard came not only from the guitar, but also from my heart. Melodies poured out of my heart, melodies I could put to those sad words I was writing.

I wrote about how sad life was, how lonely, how a woman longs for love. I'd write about happiness and how I wished life could be happy. As I watched our little girls play in our backyard I'd strum that guitar and make up sad country songs. Babysitting and guitar-picking are tied up together in my memories of those early songwriting days.

Our neighbor, Don Woodard, heard some of those songs and thought they were good. Don used to play golf with Porter Wagoner, so he told him about the songs I was writing. One day Porter Wagoner came to our house and not only liked the songs I'd written, but liked my voice too.

"I can tell a voice that's real a mile away," Porter said. "Your voice is sincere, clear, and real. Would you maybe be interested in singing and traveling?"

Of course, I had to say I couldn't, because I had two little babies, but Porter Wagoner thrilled my heart when he offered to take my songs to Chet Atkins. I gave him two or three of my early ones to show Chet Atkins.

I don't remember if my hopes were high, or what. But several days later, Porter Wagoner got in touch with me. Chet Atkins liked my songs, but said they weren't hits. He felt I was capable of writing a hit song, however, so he wanted to listen to those I wrote in the future.

The funny thing is, I wasn't trying to write "hits" and had no way of knowing whether my songs were any good or not. I simply wrote to express my deepest feelings and my pain. I had to let my sorrow out, had to express my emotions, and was simply trying to ease my poor backslidden heart. I had no songwriting ambitions, and it was another full year before I even picked up that guitar and wrote any more.

Locked in Fear

Life began to seesaw between good feelings—our little girls, homemaking duties, songwriting—and the increasing realities of ugliness, anger, and violence. When you are violated by the one who should love you most, your humanity is violated, and you are ashamed. I know how such women feel. From woman to battered woman, the feelings are nearly identical.

People ask, "Why don't you get out of it?" I don't know. For one thing, you married, intending that it should be for always. You have a vision of how marriage should be, how a home should feel, what you want for your children. You want home, church, children, your husband, and kindness. You want the goodness and security of those things.

Somewhere in your life, you keep on stubbornly clinging to those ideas, even when new patterns of violence set in. You believe his contrite words and tell yourself, *I'll try again. I must be doing things that make him act like this.* In fact, as the episodes increase, you tell yourself, *I must be a terrible person. He says it's my fault. I make him get so angry.*

You get yourself locked into the most terrible way of life, and your children are locked in with you. They live in fear. By now you are afraid to change, because you're scared of the future. You're failing as a wife, yet how in the world can you make it without this man, his good job, the wonderful house and lifestyle he provides? So you try harder and harder to please him, believe every sorry thing he says about you, and still you don't see any real answers. Without Jesus Christ, you stray further and further away from reality and His truth. You don't measure yourself against the Word of God, but believe the words of man, even when you know he is not on your side. If you stop and think for even one moment, you'd realize that God is *always* on your side, even when others are not.

Pretty soon you get used to a husband's insults and know not to answer back. Then one day, you realize you must. You talk back in that kind of situation and really set yourself up for a beating. It always happens, and it's always your fault.

Even in this apparently hopeless situation, God was stirring in my life. I did not realize it and did not make space for Him, but He was always there, even at the very worst moments of my life.

The Melody in My Heart

I had begun to write songs that people told me were good, and I thought I was the one doing it. I didn't stop to think that from the time God put music in my heart, He never took it out.

Now I see His mercy throughout every circumstance of my life, and if your life is similar to how hopeless mine was then, I pray you may come to understand that Jesus knows and cares about you.

free

VERSE 1:
I used to love to sing an old sad song,
I'd sing all day and cry all night long;
I tried to be something I never could be,
Then I met a Man who took my troubles away from me.

CHORUS:
Jesus is His name, and the word's called free;
I ain't ever been the same since His love touched me.
Just like a bird in a big oak tree,
I got a new feelin' in my soul, and the word's called free.

VERSE 2:
Free from trouble, free from pain,
Free from a sad song, I'm free from shame;
Yes, Jesus made me something I never could be,
He put a new feeling in my soul, and the word's called free.

—BETTY JEAN ROBINSON

10

Free

Many times in my life I felt different from other people, someone other people often seemed to find hard to understand. I felt different from my blonde sisters and blonde brother with their Scotch-Irish heritage. Maybe I felt different because of my heritage of Native American Indian blood.

I never minded, but the feeling of somehow being different can make you feel lonely and left out. I felt as if I marched to the beat of a different drummer. I have learned that those strange feelings are shared by many others, and usually they don't know how to handle those emotions either.

Those who have talent and sensitivity to write books or songs, those who play and sing music—I've always believed such people have emotions that can get almost like a tight-strung fiddle, so sensitive they can easily snap. You draw them too tight and one may break.

So I believe those who write or paint and make music can often live on the side of emotional danger. Since they are willing to use every human emotion to its fullest extent, creative people often don't understand that only God can put everything in its right place.

A Place on Music Row

I was to become a very successful songwriter. Bob Jennings, who headed the Four Star Music Company, heard my song, "Baby's Back Again." It was the first song I wrote for Connie Smith, and because of that song he took an interest in me.

Pictures of songwriters and famous country singers lined the walls of Four Star Music. Anything seemed possible as I studied those walls and realized those singers were always looking for a hit song, always hoping to find the big one. And Four Star wanted me on contract so they could hold an option on any future songs I might write.

So, without my hardly even trying, never dreaming I might make it, I found myself with a full-fledged songwriting contract with a publisher on Nashville's famous Music Row. My publisher, Joe Johnson, was a wonderful man, already very famous in the music world, both in Music City and far beyond. Four Star had been responsible for such hits as "Please Release Me," and the company produced many number-one songs. He produced many a great artist, but he also had a great stable of songwriters and I felt honored to be among them.

Carl Belew, one of Four Star's songwriters, wrote "What's He Doing in My World?," "Am I That Easy to Forget?," and "Heartbreak Hotel"—songs that Elvis Presley recorded. He wrote dozens of other songs for Four Star, and I learned that's what Four Star wanted its writers to do.

Every song you write can't hit the top of the charts, but you keep writing and dreaming of that number-one song. Most aspiring songwriters never even get a song heard by a producer. They come to town with a few words written on a piece of paper and they don't even get in a producer's door. They're sold everything they had just to get the money to come to Music City, and many leave broken—or they stay, and some end up on drugs and alcohol.

Joe Johnson was easy to work for and never put pressure on his writers. Whether or not you came up with a new song, you got paid each week. He respected his writers' talents and never forced them or pressured them in any way. He felt as though creative people respected their own work enough to bring forth their best, so his writers always seemed to want to do their best for Joe. I know I did.

Bob Jennings and Joe Johnson published and produced some of the top songs on Nashville's Music Row during the years I worked with them, and they did all in their power to help me become successful. I worked steadily.

The years with Four Star were those in which I guess I received everything I thought I wanted. After everything else in your life fails, you have to reach out for something, and it seemed to me that this new success must be what I was destined to discover. By now I only wanted the world to like me and my work. I started reaching out, hoping Nashville producers would think my songs were great and let their top artists record them.

A big old box of photographs from those years remind me of all the glitter. There's me, Betty Jean, wearing a big smile and all dressed up, surrounded by smiling celebrities whose faces you'd probably recognize. We were all smiling, but only God knows how much heartbreak existed in all of us.

I wrote "Red Rose From the Blue Side of Town" for George Morgan, Lorrie Morgan's dad, who was a famous Grand Old Opry singer of years ago. That was his final recorded hit, and I always thought it was the prettiest song I ever wrote. All my songs were "clean," never about whiskey, adultery, or anything else that was dirty.

In 1974 I co-wrote, with Eileen Minich, Hank Snow's last hit song, "Hello, Love." That song became number one on three industry charts—*Record World, Cash Box,* and *Billboard*—all in the same week!

That song still exists today, famous for being Garrison Keilor's theme song on his public radio program, "The Prairie Home Companion," about Lake Woebegone. By 1974 I'd had many of my songs recorded by such artists as Charlie Pride, Connie Smith, Carl Smith, Johnny Cash, George Morgan, and Hank Snow to name a few. Hank Snow recorded many of my songs, but "Hello, Love" was the biggest.

Free

In 1974 *Billboard* Magazine voted Betty Jean Robinson top female songwriter of the year. That was a terribly exciting honor. I had achieved my main ambition during those backslidden years—becoming a number-one country songwriter. *If I could achieve that,* I thought, *I could achieve happiness.* Even if my life did not change, I soon found that success and fame only made me feel more empty and lonely inside. The smiles I wore in those photographs were sad smiles, not real ones. You see, only Jesus can satisfy a soul, and my soul was not satisfied. The honors the world bestows don't matter at all when you lay your head on your pillow at night with the light out, facing yourself.

As I faced Betty Jean, I realized that all the loneliness, emptiness, anger, and despair I'd ever known in that house still were there. My number-one song didn't bring me any real happiness whatever. Oh, it brought applause and attention and some money. It brought empty honors, things that don't hold fast, and I couldn't fool myself any longer. I knew the difference between the real and the fake, and this was not real happiness.

The music world in Nashville is a strange world, I long ago began to realize. Behind all the glitter of rhinestones, there's a river of tears. Behind the fancy clothes and fine cars and homes are a million crushed hearts.

By now we had built one of those beautiful homes in Brentwood, not far from Dolly Parton's house. Our house had a winding staircase, polished floors, music room, and a beautiful barn where the girls kept their horses.

That house, which spoke of riches and success, held all the pain any heart can stand. So our family kept on going the way we were. Harry wanted me to write campaign songs for Nashville's Mayor Briley, and others, and I did. And then I got a recording contract with Metro Media, an important contract, because to sign on as both a songwriter and a singer is a real feather in any artist's hat.

A Squandered Inheritance

Our lives were progressing to a climax, but I never noticed. They signed Carl Belew and me to appear in Las Vegas, where we'd sing together. Like me, Carl Belew had Indian heritage. He was a very talented, brooding man who could say so much in just a few words. We had recorded a song I wrote called "All I Need Is You," singing it as a duet for Decca Records with Joe Johnson as our producer.

That recording jumped to the charts right away. I wrote nearly a complete album of songs for Carl Belew and me to sing together. So off Carl and I went to Las Vegas, to the Golden Nugget. Oh, the emptiness! My heart was not in Las Vegas. The Lord, I now realize, was apprehending me in the middle of all that emptiness and glitter. Right at the height of all I thought I wanted, my dear Savior was saying, "Look around you, oh prodigal child. Look around. You have squandered your inheritance. You left your

Father's house, and you are in the world, that country music world. You have squandered your inheritance."[1]

I didn't actually hear Him at that time, but He must have spoken to my heart very quietly, because I took my Bible with me. I wouldn't enter the casino after Carl and I finished singing. I never smoked, drank, or took drugs in all my life. Thank God I never took up those habits, even as a backslider.

When we'd finish a show I would head back to my room and just hold my Bible, lay it on my bed. I don't actually remember reading it, but I'd hold it in my hands, close to me. Somewhere a quiet voice was calling me, and my heart must have heard it from far, far away. *Come home, come home, child. You are weary. Oh ye who are weary, come home. Softly and tenderly Jesus is calling . . . calling, oh little back-slidden child, come home.*

I felt so terribly tired and weary. Every night I'd call home. When I left Las Vegas, I felt this terrible need to connect with my home. I was weeping. I wept every night. I wept my way back from Las Vegas, not understanding what in the world was happening.

Silent Screams

At last I got back to my beautiful home in Brentwood, that fashionable Nashville suburb with all the glamorous houses and successful people, as the world sees it. I came home so terribly weary that I could hardly wait to lie down in my pretty bed.

Then something very strange came over me. I

could not speak. I was totally paralyzed, unable to move a muscle. My eyes were wide open and staring, and my family was standing around the bed wondering what in the world was wrong. I began to scream, but not a sound came out.

Inside my chest, one scream followed another, yet I made no sound. Do you know why I was crying out? Because I was full of fear. As I lay there, I cried out from my heart. "Oh God," I said—how long it had been since I said, "Oh God!"—"Oh God, am I dying?"

The pain in my chest grew stronger as I fought my terror. Of course no sound came from the silent screams inside my chest as I said, "God, I'm dying." Suddenly my eyes fell on the ceiling above my antique dresser in the corner of the room, where a light seemed to be shining. I looked, but could not move; my eyes locked on that golden light as I lay there paralyzed and speechless.

Silently, I cried out again. "God, I'm dying. I *am* dying, aren't I, Lord? And Lord, I'm not ready to meet You." I had not thought such thoughts or said such words for nearly twenty years, but now, unable to speak aloud, I tried urgently to make Him hear me.

Immediately, from out of that golden light, a voice came into my heart—not an audible voice, but one I could hear in my heart. His voice answered, "No, child, you are not ready to meet Me."

I could only answer, "Oh, Lord!"

I lay on that bed for days. Every bone and muscle in my body felt sore. I don't know what happened to me, but I lay there too tired and weak to get up, just

(LEFT) *"This is my senior High-school picture from Bell County High. I was surprised when they voted me the prettiest girl in the class of '53."*

(RIGHT) *"My boss, a great American, former FBI director, J. Edgar Hoover."*

"I became Miss D. C. Poppy Queen and met President Nixon."

"While I was working for the FBI in Washington D. C., I met my husband, Harry Robinson. But deep in my heart, I always longed to go home. I never forgot my Holiness roots."

"I had begun to write songs that people told me were good, and I thought I was the one doing it. I didn't stop to think that from the time God put music in my heart, He never took it out."

"Daddy was baptized one month before he went home to be with the Lord . . . I was back in Nashville far from God at the time. How I wish I could have been there."

Betty Jean receives the Songwriter of the Year award from Bob Jenning of Four-Star Music (LEFT) and DJ Beff Collie (RIGHT).

(TOP) *Here Betty Jean is with Jerry Chestnut and Eddie Miller.*
Eddie wrote the song, "Release Me."

❧ ❧ ❧

(BELOW) *Betty Jean with some of country music's greatest — Dolly*
Parton, Tom T. Hall, J. Marijon Wilkins, and Eddie Miller.

"One day I just got on my knees and said, 'Jesus, if You will, please receive me back. I promise I'll serve You the rest of my life.'"

"As I spoke those words, the joy of my salvation immediately sprang up fresh, and He restored my soul."

"The Lord had healed me, had healed me so that now I could love. Jesus gave me the baptism of love as only Jesus can. Thank You, Lord."

"My friends in Jesus' work—Trinity Broadcasting Network president, Paul Crouch (LEFT) and his wife, Jan (CENTER). I have been with TBN since the 70s."

(LEFT) *"Here I am with Dean Crigger, a true servant of God and a friend. He is a talented musician, songwriter, and manager for Melody Mountain Records."*

(**Above, left to right**) *George, Betty Jean, Martha Belle (behind Betty Jean), Hala, and Lucy Mae. This picture was taken in Straight Creek in Hala's garden.*

❧ ❧ ❧

(**Below, left to right**) *Betty Jean's family: Joshua James, Sunday, daughter Rebecca, Rachel Haley, Betty Jean, Annie Gray, daughter Elizabeth Kimberly, and Hadassah.*

Betty Jean's first schoolhouse and the church Papa Rhodes attended. (LEFT TO RIGHT) Betty Jean, Hala Rhodes, and Martha Belle.

(LEFT) Betty Jean's present home in Straight Creek, Kentucky.

(BELOW) Today Betty Jean writes and sings for Jesus.

❧

Up on Melody Mountain

❧❧

lay there for days. During that time I thought much about the fruitless life I had lived for nearly twenty years. I did not think of the hell I lived in, just about how futile my life had been. I realized fully and deeply that I had not lived for the Lord for a long, long time.

God had allowed me to see that when I left the mountains of Kentucky I had left Jesus behind. He never left me, but I departed from Him. For days I lay in my bed thinking about that.

A Disintegrating Family

I began to look toward my heavenly home. But when I arose from my bed and resumed my normal life, I was in that same stressful home I had endured for years. When I began attending church again, taking Rebecca and Kimberly with me, things grew radically worse.

Rebecca was always a sweet and gentle child that never gave me any trouble until she was a teenager, but she seemed to be in her own world. Rebecca already was into rebellion and running with the wrong crowd.

Kimberly loved her horses and spent a lot of time in our beautiful barn with her horse, Lady. Or she closed herself up in her lovely bedroom. Rebecca, a beautiful blonde child, cared nothing for her room, or for anything else, as far as I could tell. But Kimberly, the girl who loved nature and the world outside, the girl who never gave me a problem, always escaped to her room whenever Daddy was mean to Mama. She would close the door and look out into the meadows where she could see the barn and Lady, her horse.

Our house those days was like so many others—beautiful, refined, and polished, but inside there was every problem Satan could think of. Harry and I had begun to pull in different directions. My husband would buy our daughters Alice Cooper and David Bowie tapes, rock music that I couldn't stand, and he made sure they attended every concert when these "stars" came to Nashville.

I wouldn't go. So we pulled apart, one liking rock music and the other not; one using profanity, the other not; one who believed in social drinking, one who did not. Even if you are not a Christian and not with the Lord, if one spouse doesn't like that stuff and the other spouse does, you're in trouble. The head of the house has much influence on his children, for better or worse.

So, Elizabeth Kimberly would hide in her room where she could pretend that the violence wasn't happening, that her daddy never attacked her mama. And Rebecca would go out with her friends, go on her party way. Each did her best to escape, each in her own way.

Soul-struggles were taking place in that lovely Brentwood home where very little love ever got expressed. Not openly, but quietly, Satan pitted one parent against the other in a terrible, unspoken contest. Who would control Becky's and Kimberly's futures . . . their very souls? What would they believe? Would they reject God, or come to know Him?

Free

I had to find a church. Soon the three of us began attending a nearby Baptist church, one that was much more formal than any other I'd ever attended. But that didn't matter. I felt so empty in that church. They didn't believe in guitars. They found out I could sing, and asked me to sing some of the old songs such as "Life's Railway to Heaven," or "Lord, I'm Coming Home." But my soul grew more and more hungry and unsatisfied.

Home at Last!

Then came the weekend when Harry went on a fishing trip with his friends. That Sunday the girls and I drove across Antioch, and I saw this little bitty church, its front doors flung wide open, and the people inside praising God with their hands raised towards heaven.

How many years, Lord, since I saw that . . . those raised hands . . . and the years suddenly flew backward in my mind as my heart filled with memories of Straight Creek and my Holiness people, all of us lifting our hands, glorifying and worshiping God. I stopped the car right beside that little church and went in there with my children.

Betty Jean Robinson at that moment was at the height of her professional career, a well-known, award-winning songwriter and singer. But that's not the Betty Jean who entered that tiny church. The Betty Jean who tremblingly found a pew in that church where they lifted their hands and their hearts to Jesus in true praise was the same young girl who had walked the railroad track to Brother and Sister Lankford's house, standing on spiritual tiptoes, so eager to enter the presence of the Lord.

I sat there and listened, listened to Brother Driver preach and Sister Driver play the organ. This was an Assembly of God church, a denomination I'd never heard of. But I liked it, and I sat there and allowed the Lord Himself to fill my cup, offering the water of life to this poor parched and dying soul.

I was on my way back to my Father's house. I was about to learn how to be free.

Endnote

1. See Luke 15:11–24.

I Turned It Over to Jesus

VERSE 1:
Scarred and bruised by a cruel world,
Rejected, forgotten and alone,
No one to love me, no one to care,
Out drifting on my own,
Then out of the darkness I saw a light
Break through like a new day's dawn.
My chains fell off when He lifted me up,
And He held me until the pain was all gone.

CHORUS:
I turned it over to Jesus
And oh, the peace I found
When I turned it all over to Jesus,
He turned my life around.

RECITATION:
Oh, you've searched for happiness all your life,
and you've not found it. You've tried drugs, and
you've turned to alcohol. Why, you even sell your
own body trying to buy peace of mind. And you cry,
oh, God, I can't go on another day. Oh, listen to me.
Please, won't you listen to me right now. You can't
buy peace of mind. But I can point you to One who
paid the price for your peace of mind. His name is
Jesus Christ, the son of the almighty God. If you'll
just turn to Him right now, listen, He'll give you
that peace that you've never had before.

REPEAT:
Why don't you turn it all over to Jesus,

CHORUS:
And let Him turn your life all around?

—BETTY JEAN ROBINSON

11

I Turned It Over to Jesus

At that point I still had not turned it all over to Jesus, so Satan, seeing a wide-open opportunity in my life, hit me with two of his cruelest blows. Each nearly killed me; the first, physically; the second, with grief for one of my children.

One day I woke up terribly ill and had to be rushed to Vanderbilt Hospital. They discovered I was pregnant, but it was a tubular pregnancy, so of course could never come to term. After emergency surgery and seven days of life-threatening illness, pain, and grief, they brought me home to a strange-feeling house.

Something obviously was going on, but in my sick, groggy state I could not tell what. Harry came in and out, hurrying from one part of the house to another, and wouldn't tell me anything. At last I insisted that he give me the facts—and they were horrifying.

One day at school Kimberly, then eleven, suffered a terrible freak accident. The teacher had not arrived and the classroom door was locked, so they decided to boost Kimberly, who was tiny, through a partially opened window so she could enter the room and unlock the door.

Nobody knew the janitor had been working on a loose window pane in that window and had left it in the frame. When Kimberly touched it, the glass fell out and cut off her nose. It had just happened, and poor Harry was trying to deal with that trauma and not upset his still sick wife. He must have felt almost crazy.

Kimberly had been rushed to Vanderbilt Hospital, where the doctors ordered someone to return to the school to try to find her nose. Praise God, they did find it in the hot sun—it was May, just before school let out—but the principal, who was real wise, had been in the army and knew what to do. He knew that if you put an appendage in its own blood, it can live. So he put it in a blood-soaked paper towel, rushed it to the hospital, and the doctors sewed that little turned-up nose back on her face.

Kimberly would experience several years of plastic surgery, pain, and trauma before she became healed, but God was faithful. Meanwhile, my daughter suffered from her disfigurement, the bandages, and her schoolmates' careless, often cruel remarks. She also needed pain medication all those years, which was to become the greatest stumbling block of her life—prescription drugs, which set up a dependency.

I Turned It Over to Jesus

Meanwhile, amid all these concerns, Becky's teenage rebellion and my husband's increasing anger and violence made life almost unbearable. And the music which once had given me release, now seemed empty and pointless.

Precious Times in a Little Church

But I kept going to that Assembly of God church, sometimes going almost out of desperation. Harry didn't want me taking the girls to church. I couldn't do any more than I was doing. In fact, my husband did everything he could to thwart my own church attendance, pouring beer over my head after I was dressed for church, for example.

Kimberly kept on going to church with me, and I kept on calling out to God. I wanted to do something for the Lord, for His church, so I'd be the first to volunteer to clean the building. I'd vacuum the aisles, and dust the pews, and set flowers around to make the sanctuary pretty. Now and then I'd run to the altar and kneel down, because I had the sanctuary to myself and was free to pray. Sometimes I could hear the preacher praying in his study as he prepared the Sunday sermon.

Those were precious times in that little church that held one hundred and twenty-five souls, but was available to me for a private sanctuary during the hours I roamed up and down the aisles, dusting and praying. After I worked awhile I'd run down the aisle, kneel at the altar, and sing a song I hadn't thought of since I was in the church in Straight Creek.

That beautiful song came back to me, and I thought, *Lord, I used to love this song. Thank You for bringing it back to me*, and I'd sing,

Jesus, use me, and, oh, Lord, don't refuse me,
For surely there's a work I can do;
And even though it's humble, Lord, help my will to
    crumble,
And though the cost be great, I'll work for You.

I had no idea what the cost of discipleship might be in that home of ours, but I knew that song was ringing in my heart. *Though the cost be great, I'll work for You.*

Meanwhile, as I'd pray, "Lord Jesus, have mercy on me," the devil would say, "You can't come back to God. You've sinned too much. God don't know where you are." Then I'd think, *Lord if I'm good, maybe if I'm good, the Lord will take me back.* I thought that by works, by my own "goodness," I could get God's attention and approval, and my soul could be restored.

I longed to return to my Father's house, and I hoped my good works would get me there. But you and I can never be good enough, for only Jesus is truly good. As you look to Jesus, turning to Him, He pours His goodness into you and through you. His is the goodness, and there is no other. The Bible says our goodness is as filthy rags compared to that One who is pure, perfect, and holy.[1] When we have Him we have all we need. Thank You, Jesus.

I Turned It Over to Jesus

Oh, the Joy!

As I tried to work my way back to the Lord, the devil made sure he laid condemnation on me. I would fall into discouragement and say, "Oh God, I'll never get back." The devil was beating me over the head with condemnation.

But one day I walked through the fire. I called out to my Lord Jesus in my kitchen, there by the old oak table, and it was so simple. I just got on my knees and said, "Jesus, if You will, please receive me back. I promise I'll serve You the rest of my life. If I fall and falter, if I fail You, I'll get back up on my feet, Lord. I won't take my eyes off You, but will just keep walking toward You."

As I spoke those words, the joy of His salvation immediately sprang up fresh, and He restored my soul. Joy I hadn't felt in years flooded over me, and every chain and burden fell away. Oh, the joy! I was filled with inexpressible joy, and could hardly wait to go back to the house of the Lord.

The more I loved Jesus, of course, the worse it became in my home. Some of you have had the same kinds of persecution after you came to the Lord, the end of a heavy boot kicking you while you're down praying, or a hateful voice calling you bad names. Maybe you've been pushed out of your door, shoved off the porch to fall several feet to the ground, locked out of your house. That devil can't stand the Holy Ghost.

A Great Battle

One evening when every window and door in the house was locked against me, I went to the barn loft to sleep. Just as I once had sat with Mammy in the loft where she rested and prayed, now it was my time to find a retreat where I could seek the Lord. Little did I know I was about to enter into the most awesome battle of my life, when the devil absolutely tried to stop me.

I climbed the ladder to the loft where the hay was stored, a nice breezy place where I'd hung strings of onions from my garden to dry. I knelt before a bale of hay, placed my elbows there to balance myself, and began to pray to God. Immediately I was aware of a Presence, as real as could be, and I knew that the Lord Jesus Himself or one of His angels stood at my right side, beside that bale of hay.

Meanwhile, a spirit of darkness appeared on my left side, pulling at me, pulling me, trying to draw me back and away from God. But that blessed sweet Spirit, the Spirit of God, stood at my right side as the awesome confrontation began. I could not tell you today what went on in my heart and mind at that moment, what I intended to pray or speak, but suddenly out of the depths of my heart an old Baptist song I sang years earlier rose up and burst out of my lips. In my own innocence, not knowing how to fight Satan or use God's Word against the enemy, I simply began to sing:

> I will arise and go to Jesus, and He will embrace me in His arms.

I Turned It Over to Jesus

In the arms of my sweet Savior, oh there are
ten thousand charms.

As I sang, that old spirit of darkness threw his
cloak over his head and fled away, and my Savior
was there to minister to me with His angels.

After that experience, that powerful encounter
with God, I was able to face the trials that came
upon me. I started writing songs again. When I could
return to the house and to my music room, I wrote
my first gospel song. Actually it was my second, if
you count the one I wrote as a teenage girl, but this
was the first I recorded.

Little did I dream that the song coming out of my
lips and through my fingers as they strummed the
guitar would become my ministry's theme song,
known to thousands and millions of people over the
world who have heard me sing it. That day I could
not conceive that there would be a ministry some
day, or other gospel songs, or even the simple joys of
everyday life. I was still struggling at home, and had
no idea how any of it would turn out.

But God knew. He knew as my fingers roamed
over the guitar strings, as words came into my mind
and formed themselves into verses. He knew the out-
come of my life, sure as He knew the words to my
new song. "Jesus is coming," I began, "Can't you see
it everywhere? This old world's rumbling, can't you
feel it in the air? Neighbor, tell your neighbor, flee the
wrath to come. It's time to get started on the way
home."

On the Way Home

About that time Joe Johnson, my producer and friend, sent for me. "Betty Jean, it's time for you to do another record," he said. We released two a year, and I knew it was time for the next one, but I didn't feel like singing the kind of songs I used to write.

I took a tape of that little song I'd just written, the only gospel song I had, and went to see this powerful producer, Joe Johnson, in his sophisticated offices in Nashville's Music Row. I entered Joe's office suite wondering what in the world would happen but determined not to sing any more country songs. To me it was real clear-cut; now that I knew Jesus, I should sing His songs.

Normally I would have brought a pack of new songs to present to Joe Johnson for his inspection. So I sat down beside his desk, with that one little tape in my pocketbook, and began, "Joe . . ."

Before I could go on, Joe Johnson interrupted. "Betty Jean," he said, knowing nothing of all the recent events in my life, "I feel as though you should sing a different type of song. You should go in a different direction." That kind, dear man didn't know exactly what he was trying to say, how to describe what he wanted, but I instantly understood that the Lord was speaking through my wonderful friend. I picked up the guitar that producers always have leaning against their desks, hit the key of A, and began singing "Jesus Is Coming."

When I got to the end of that new song, I looked up and saw tears in Joe's eyes. He said, "This is the kind of song you should be singing." We got up and went into a recording studio where some of Nashville's top musicians were working, they sat down, and we began playing. As we played that song, something happened in the studio.

Neither the musicians nor Joe sensed exactly what was happening, but we all knew something was different. They kept talking about that song, trying to describe what was there, not knowing how to identify whatever about it was touching them so.

Joe released "On the Way Home" as the A side of a record, and it ended up on the country charts. Several country artists wanted to record it. Because of recording-studio politics, some say the record should have gone much higher on the charts, but I didn't care about that. By now I was in love with Jesus. He was all that mattered to me.

Harry

I had begun to sing only gospel music. One evening, over a late supper, my husband asked, "Is this the kind of music you're going to sing from now on?"

"Yes, Harry," I answered, "This is the kind of music I'm going to sing." The Holy Spirit must have come and brought peace, because my husband didn't get angry with me. He sat and ate and listened quietly as I talked to him about his soul. I told Harry what Jesus had done for me and what He would do for him. He sat there and looked at me for a long time, listened, and was very quiet as though he had been captured by the presence of the Lord and didn't know how to explain it.

After a long time of looking at me thoughtfully, and just listening, my husband suddenly got real angry. "If that's the way you're going, I'm not going with you," he said. "You're not going with me, and I'm not going with you." Angrily, he pushed away from the table and stormed out of the room.

That was to be the first of many new confrontations and fits of anger from Harry toward me. Sometimes I literally saw the face of the enemy upon my husband's countenance.

During the next months, knowing that my husband would not stand for me living for the Lord, I knew I had something important to deal with. After you come to the Lord He brings things to the surface, things buried deep in your life. God knew I had held resentment against my husband for the way he treated me, and God would not let that thing go undealt with. He knew I couldn't harbor such resentment in my heart.

One day when Harry was playing golf, I went into my bedroom and knelt by my bed. I didn't know how to pray what I needed to pray, but I began crying out to God. "Lord, I want to love this man . . . I want to love my husband . . . no matter what he has done to me, I want to love him again. I want to be able to totally forgive him, Lord."

I cried out to Jesus, and didn't know but one way to cry. I had once heard Brother David Wilkerson say, "Jesus will give you a baptism of love." So I cried out, "Jesus, will You give me love? Will You give me love?"

It was as though my heart and soul were wrung

out like a dishrag. That thing buried so deep down there, that resentment, my unforgiveness, came up and out of me as Jesus wrung me apart. Oh, how it hurt.

When my blessed Savior took His knife and cut into my heart with His love, He cut the core of all that resentment and unforgiveness out of my heart and threw it away forever. When He did, He poured His love into my heart and filled it to overflowing. All the hurts and terrible feelings I'd ever had, He forgave. All the hurts and terrible things I'd suffered from Harry, I forgave.

I don't know how long I lay there, prostrate before God on my bedroom floor, but when I came to, I felt like Sister Lankford. I felt as if I could take the whole world and wrap my arms around it, that I could love all my enemies and could hug those who had hurt me the most.

All at once I heard the kitchen door rattling, so I ran in there and it was him—my husband. At that moment, the Lord dealt with me about myself. He let me see myself clearly, and I went into the kitchen and said to Harry, "Will you forgive me? Please forgive me if I ever have hurt you, or if I ever said anything to displease you." He looked absolutely astounded.

Set Free

And at that moment I was set free. Now I could truly love, could replace all those years of hurt and pain with love. The Lord had healed me, had healed me so that now I could love. Jesus gave me the baptism of love as only Jesus can. Thank You, Lord.

The Lord will change you only when you turn everything over to Him. And when you change, the situation around you will change. It's amazing. There may be many sorrows ahead—many mountains, valleys, and stony places to climb—but you're headed toward pure sunshine. You're headed toward a life that's worth living, that's worth something in the kingdom of God. Your life will become a living testimony, and God will lead you into whatever He wants you to do to bring glory to Him.

The change in me was so great, my joy so full, my ability to love so freed up, that I believed great things for my husband. I prayed for him, and the precious people in our church prayed with me. We all prayed, fasted, and believed God for my husband's salvation.

God sent Fran and Barker Harrison, two of the most precious friends I ever had, to stand with me. He always will do that, send other loving saints to help you fight your battles when you need human arms around you.

However, nothing changed. After my bearing many bitter episodes, walking with God and continuing in love, my husband abandoned me and our girls and took someone else. In my sorrow and hurt, depression fell over my life. I feared the future. I felt overwhelmed by our physical and financial needs. To be alone, to be abandoned, was a scary thing, and I'd wake up in the morning terrified and depressed. That's no way for a Christian to face life, but the battle was raging so strong. I'd sleep in my music room rather than be alone in my bedroom.

One morning I got out of my bed in the music

I Turned It Over to Jesus

room and walked over to the window, where the Lord spoke to my heart. I feel that what He told me that day is what someone reading this book needs to hear. God said, "I will make the thorns that are under your feet as soft as the petals of a rose. I am that rose, and its petals are My blood."

He said, "When your eyes look down, My child, your enemy will seek to break you. From the dawn of each morning keep My name before you, and utter praises to Me."

Do you know what else He said? He said, "You are precious to Me. I watch you with eyes that never look away."

The next morning when I awakened I felt I could hear angels singing over my bed:

Victory in Jesus, my Savior, forever,
He sought me and bo't me with His redeeming blood;
He loved me ere I knew Him, and all my love is due Him,
He plunged me to victory beneath the cleansing flood.[2]

From that moment until today, I never again awakened in depression. No matter how many things Satan sets against me, I can awaken with the sweet name of Jesus on my lips. Thank You, sweet Jesus, and good morning, Lord. I love You, Jesus.

Endnotes

1. See Isaiah 64:6.
2. Text and music by Eugene M. Bartlett, Sr. Copyright © 1939 by E. M. Bartlett. Copyright © 1967 by Mrs. E. M. Bartlett, Renewal. Assigned to Albert E. Brumley & Sons. All rights reserved. Used by permission.

Resting in the Lord

CHORUS:
I'm just resting in the Lord today,
I'm just resting in the Lord today;
My victory came this morning when I knelt to pray,
I'm just resting in the Lord today.

VERSE 1:
Had my battles with ol' Satan all week long,
He tried to steal my joy and take my song;
But victory came this morning when I knelt to pray.
I'm just resting in the Lord today.

VERSE 2:
I was tempted, I was tested, I was tried,
But I said, "Ol' Satan, get behind me with all your lies."
For the Holy Ghost will keep me as I go on my way,
I'm just resting in the Lord today.

—BETTY JEAN ROBINSON

12

Resting in the Lord

When the sheriff brought divorce papers to the house, I didn't know what to do. "What are these?" I asked, and he answered me so rough and cruel.

Stunned, I called my pastor. He said, "Let's pray," knowing there'd be thirty days before the divorce could be final. We prayed and waited on the Lord, but nothing changed. My husband went through with the divorce.

The abandonment and sorrow felt terrible. It felt as if I had an empty place in my heart. Still, I thought, *Maybe he will get saved and come back to us.* Even though our marriage had been awful, this abandonment felt worse. I had no idea what might lie ahead.

"Lord, Fill This Empty Place"

One day I got in my car and drove and prayed. "Lord, please fill up this hole in my heart with Your love. Only You know what will happen to us, and I depend on You. This abandonment hurts so bad. Please fill me with Your love." There in that car, the Lord God filled me with what I needed—Him and His love. He poured His love into me and filled that hole up, filled it to overflowing, and has kept it filled ever since.

Once Jesus pours His love out on you, it fills all the empty places in your life. He'll never take it back; that love is yours forever. Remember, He promised, "I will never leave you nor forsake you."[1] He told us to cast all our care on Him.[2] He said, "I am with you always, even unto the end of the world."[3]

That same day I discovered the house I live in now. You see, I knew I had to leave that big old Brentwood home that I would not be able to afford, and that I'd better find some tiny house. My faith wasn't large enough to imagine anything nice. It didn't stretch to material things. So I thought, *Since I'm not singing country music any more, I'll never be able to afford anything much.*

The house God led me to was a split-level, which I didn't care for, and had been unoccupied for about two years. The owners had reduced and reduced the price because the house looked as abandoned as I felt. It wasn't large or beautiful, and I had no desire toward it whatever. But surrounding that little old house I saw the most beautiful acreage, wonderful stands of trees, stone fences laid long ago by the colonists, and wild creatures living in the woods. My heart reached out and got tangled up in those tree-tops, soared like those birds in the trees. I bought the property, not for the house but for the fields and trees. All the years my husband and I had worked to keep nice houses, we had lived on streets that had been cleared of most trees. Now the Lord had returned me at last to the environment my soul needed, a wooded place filled with His peace and beauty.

So I made up my mind to go live in that cove where you could see straight up into the mountains, and live in that modest house. And while I was yet packing to move, the Lord gave me the most miraculous confirmation that this was His choice for me.

Run Along, Little Lamb

The moment I signed for that property, other potential buyers seemed to come out of the woodwork. Nobody had wanted it for more than two years, but the minute I decided to buy it, it seemed like others wanted it too. I was beginning to suspect that God had held out that property with Betty Jean Robinson in mind.

Before we moved in, however, a real miracle occurred. Kimberly came to me one day and said, "Mama, please let me go over to that little house so I can sit by the fireplace and read my Bible." She said, "I want to be alone."

That seemed unusual, but I took her there,

knowing the boys were teasing her, and she was suffering from the scars on her face. "Just let me take some juice and my Bible," she said, "and leave me there alone, Mama." For some reason I felt this would be all right, so I drove Kimberly to the house, lit a fire in the stone fireplace, and went back home to pack.

When I returned to get her several hours later, the happiest little girl ran out to meet me. I'd left a child there who felt so ugly and depressed over her surgical scars in the middle of her face, yet the child I picked up had a face that was absolutely shining. "Mama, Mama, let me tell you what happened," she said, very excited.

"I was sitting by the fireplace in that empty room," she began, "and I don't think I went to sleep. I think I was awake, but it felt like I was asleep." As she described what she had seen, I began to realize that little Kimberly had gotten caught up in a vision. She saw clouds circling the room, and a great throne with bells and stars around it.

"I was reading Isaiah," she told me, "and it seemed like I was asleep, but I guess I was awake. When I looked up, I saw Jesus. He had snow-white hair, and His robe was so white and shining. The throne, and Jesus, were so big they seemed to fill the room, and in one of His hands He was holding a big walking stick." I knew she meant a shepherd's staff, but I didn't interrupt what my child was telling me. "He brought me up before Him on that cloud, and I was so ragged and tattered, but I knelt there before Him, knelt down way low."

Resting in the Lord

Then Jesus spoke to her, Kimberly said, in a low voice that seemed to fill the whole universe, a gentle voice that made her feel no fear. "My little lamb, my child, tell me what's wrong," she said Jesus encouraged. "But before I could even speak, Mama, Jesus knew my thoughts. I could tell He already knew.

"His face was so shining, like a glowing light, and His eyes so bright, and He told me all that was wrong with me, everything I was feeling. He told *me* the things I wanted to tell *Him!* Then He said, 'Run along, little lamb. Always remember, when you are in trouble, come to Me.'"

Then the swirl of clouds and the throne dimmed and were gone. "I thought I was beautiful," my child told me. "I thought my nose and my face must be beautiful, so I ran upstairs and looked in the bathroom mirror, because I thought the scars would all be gone. But the scars were still there.

"I ran back downstairs to the big window that looks out over the mountain, and something ugly said to me, 'You are still ugly.'

"I said, 'No I am not. I'm not ugly anymore.'" Then Kimberly said she ran upstairs to that mirror and looked once again. "I still have my scars," she told me, "but now it doesn't make any difference."

I knew that our Lord had actually come to my child Kimberly, had visited her as she read her Bible by the light of the fire. Not all of us get to see such heavenly visions, but He is a Lord who will comfort a little child. Most of us never will see the Lord in person, but He still comforts us today.

"Blessed are they who have not seen, and yet have

believed."[4] He says that one day that we will see Him face-to-face, that glorious Savior that John the revelator saw and described in the Book of Revelation.[5]

We will be with Him one day. We will see Him and know Him. But meanwhile, He appeared in our house to my hurting child, and He healed her pain.

Gethsemane

After we moved into that new house, my own Gethsemane came. The enemy had allowed someone I trusted, someone who was helping me with my business affairs, to steal my song royalties and leave me financially destitute.

What would become of us? What could I do? Since leaving the FBI, every dime I ever made was through music, and I had turned my back on lucrative country songwriting, singing, and recording. Now my royalties had been wasted, my income totally dried up. How would we live?

I began to cry out to the Lord because I had become very scared. My faith concerning financial matters was still very weak. I guess I forgot that the Lord promises to feed the sparrows.[6] So I would cry out to Jesus, begging Him for the rent money, because I had to make house payments now. *And Lord, what about the telephone bill?* So I cried and travailed before the Lord for such things, weeping because I didn't know where the next house payment was coming from.

The enemy, of course, found this a good time to tempt me. I began receiving phone calls from Music

Row, top recording companies, saying, "Come on back." Joe Johnson, gentleman that he is, had released me from his contract, and I guess word had gotten out and other companies were being used by the enemy to tempt me, in my time of financial distress.

I said, "I don't sing those songs anymore." And one recording executive replied, "I know that, but you can make a gospel album once a year along with your country albums. If you want to, you can put a gospel song on every country album you cut." See what the enemy was trying to get me to do? He wanted me to compromise. But I'd made up my mind that I'd go all the way with Jesus. If I sang any songs, I was determined that they would glorify His precious name.

One by one the various record companies, including Word, so widely respected in the Christian world, flew me to Waco, Texas, to make their offers. Each time, the Lord said no. "Even this company, Lord?" In my ignorance and lack of faith, I could see my business opportunities drying up, one by one.

All I seemed to hear from God those days was, *No, you can't.* One day, in despair, I got down on my knees beside my bed. "God," I asked, "Why can't I sing gospel music? You won't give me peace to sing country music, and You won't give me peace to write and sing for big gospel labels. What am I going to do?"

Then I made a big mistake with Him as I continued to pray. "What about *her?*" I asked, naming someone who recorded both gospel and country.

And when I mentioned this person's name to Jesus, do you know what happened? The moment I mentioned another person, brought up another name to Him, it's as if He shut the heavens up and would not talk with me anymore. I felt so alone.

As I continued to kneel beside my bed, the heavens seemed to become like brass, and I thought, *Oh, Lord, please don't leave me. Don't break off communication with me, Lord. I'm already in enough trouble. Please don't go away. You're the only One I have to depend upon.*

As I prayed and waited I realized something vitally important. God deals with us *one-on-one,* and we are not to bring other names into the conversation. I felt so convicted that I knew I had to ask His forgiveness, and I did. "I'm sorry I brought up her name."

The Lord then spoke to my heart. "But child, you can't go that way. You follow Me," He said, and then He waited. You see, I was praying about the only way I knew to make a living, and it was urgent that I hear from God about it. Gradually I began to realize that I was holding this little golden box—my talent—thinking that it belonged to me, and that I had a right to use it. This thing was real precious to me, something Betty Jean was clutching tightly.

But the Lord wanted me to give it over. He wanted me to be willing to be stripped of everything, everything in the world I could lean on, so I would learn to lean entirely on Him and His provision for me. While Jesus waited to see what I would do, I took one last look at that box that contained my talents and abilities. I wrestled with myself, because I wanted to hold on to it. I was afraid to trust Jesus totally, to abandon myself to God, to give up all my personal talents and everything else I had and was. He waited, and I waited it out, as He continually said, "Follow Me."

That was my personal Gethsemane. I thought of my Savior, all He had done for me, the joy and peace He brought me. I recalled how much sadness and grief He had carried me through, had borne for my sake, and how He stayed with me and never left my side.

Jesus is more precious to me, I realized, than anything else I have ever known or experienced or owned in my life. I found it easy to say, "Lord, here it is. Here is all of me. I claim nothing for myself, Lord. And if I never sing another song, I will follow You and serve You all the days of my life."

Peace Flows In

For the first time, I had truly prayed for God's will in my life, and not my own. For the first time I could understand Jesus' prayer before He went to the cross: "Father, not My will, but Thy will be done."[7] When at last you can pray that prayer, He sends His angels to minister to you. It is settled.

No more would I question the Lord with all those reasonable ideas of mine: *Why can't I? Why do you let her? If I can't do this, how will we live?* When at last I surrendered to Him and said, "Yes, Lord, I offer everything to You," I gave Him complete authority in my life, and miracles began. Peace flowed in. The learning process commenced, and He led me day by day, hour by hour, beside the still waters.[8]

After all that was settled, I borrowed a little money from the bank and made a little private-label recording, which I entitled "Songs I Grew Up On." I included "Amazing Grace" and "Take My Hand, Precious Lord," old-time songs of comfort and faith. Gospel music people told me, "They ain't singing them kind of songs no more. They want contemporary music these days."

But my heart just wouldn't sing contemporary music. Maybe I'm too countrified for that. Anyhow, I had pledged to the Lord, "God, I'll sing what I feel I'm supposed to sing. Not what's popular, not what's commercial, but I'll sing what's in my heart, and write what my heart tells me Your precious people need to hear. I want to encourage Your blessed people, and the prisoners, and help the backsliders to come back home."

I was determined that my songs would encourage the sick, the brokenhearted, and the hopeless. I knew that the blessed name of Jesus held all the power. So I never had any desire to return to that world, that world of Nashville glitter and fame. That's the way Jesus led me, making me understand that He had an individual path for me to walk, looking neither to the left nor to the right, and not comparing His will for me to His will for anyone else.

It's not your *talent* He's interested in, but the *vessel*—you. That vessel He loves so much, not for anything you'll ever do or succeed in. Jesus simply wants to become the Lord of your life. He wants to become Lord of your dreams and plans, your hopes and ambitions—everything you possess.

I didn't know what direction the Lord would let me take, that day as I knelt beside my bed and I yielded myself totally to Him. I didn't know if I'd ever sing in public again, or did I dream that I would someday minister to His people. I only knew that I loved Him and would obey Him.

My obedience was what He needed in order to put my feet on His far more glorious path, a path far beyond anything I could ever ask or even think.[9] Praise God forever!

Endnotes

1. Hebrews 13:53.
2. See 1 Peter 5:7.
3. See Matthew 28:20.
4. John 20:20.
5. See 1 Corinthians 13:12.
6. Matthew 6:26.
7. Luke 22:42.
8. Psalm 23:2.
9. Ephesians 3:20.

Jesus, You're All to Me

VERSE 1:
When the one I trusted the most crushed my heart,
I found it so hard to forgive,
I went into my room, turned my face to the wall,
And I cried, God, I don't want to live.

VERSE 2:
No one could reach me, and very few tried,
As bitterness closed in on me;
My heart turned to marble, still I cried out deep inside,
Oh, God, is there no hope for me?

VERSE 3:
Then someone so gentle came into my room
And with a voice so tender and sweet,
He said, Child, I love you, you don't have to be afraid,
Just trust Me, for I'm all that you will ever need.

CHORUS:
Jesus, my Jesus, You came just in time;
One touch and I stood on my feet.
You're more than a rainbow, You're first in my life,
Sweet Jesus, You're all to me.

—BETTY JEAN ROBINSON

13

Jesus, You're All to Me

Living in a dream world can make us see white that's really black, and as long as I fooled myself, I found it wasn't all so bad. But my other self kept forcing bits of truth into focus. . . .

I wrote those words soon after my husband left us. Now that I had come under the protection and leadership of my Lord Jesus Christ, there would be no more dream world for me, no more pretending about certain parts of my unhappy life. Jesus said, "I am the way, the truth, and the life" . . . everything I so desperately needed.[1]

For two years after my divorce God patiently taught me to follow Him and take one day at a time, just one little bitty baby step after another. When you choose to live in a dream world, you become good at evading hard things, painful things. But when you live for Jesus, you learn that He always walks beside you, no matter how hot the fire or how overwhelming the flood.

I told you how hard it was, learning to trust God for every penny. How I used to pray and call out to God, weep, travail, and agonize over my rent. Yet somehow it always came. Once or twice I went to my mailbox and, without a name on it, found an envelope with the exact amount I needed for my house payment.

The Lord continued to show me His provision. Once when I was so troubled about finances, about how I was going to pay my monthly bills, He spoke to my heart, "Child, don't you know that I know where you are? Don't you know I could take My mighty hand and scrape off the top of that mountain and dip gold out of it if you needed it? Don't you know I own the cattle on a thousand hills? That the earth is mine, and the fullness thereof?"[2] I rejoiced as God spoke those things to my heart and urged me not to worry.

"I Will Give You This Little House"

During this time when I was learning to trust God for all my needs, I was praying one day . . . and sometimes, instead of praying, we should just be still and listen. He interrupted my prayer; He apprehended me. That quiet voice of authority said, "Get up, child—go upstairs and look out your window into the yard." The presence of the Lord came upon me, and I ran like a deer to that upstairs window. As I looked out I began to weep about my house, weep with a broken spirit in the presence of the Lord. I owed for that house; it was not yet mine.

The Lord spoke to my heart. "Betty Jean, will you give Me this house?" I thought as I looked out the window, *What a strange thing for the Lord to ask! Lord, what do You want with it? What do You want me to do?*

Then I thought, *Does He want me to have Bible studies here?* All He had asked was, "Will you give Me this house?" But I was trying to figure out what He wanted with it. *Why does God need my house?*

At last I said, "Yes, Lord. I will give You this house. I don't know what You can do with it. Why do You want it? You already own everything—but yes, Lord, I will give You this house."

At that moment something was released in me, and I began to praise and glorify God, feeling such joy, peace, and freedom. From that moment on, I never had to think about a house payment or ever again ask Him how I could find the money. The burden was lifted month by month without my even realizing it.

When you give something to God you never have to worry about it again. Now the house is paid for, and I am free of monthly payments—but what's more important, long before that happened, God taught me how to be free of each month's fear about needing money. That worry was lifted from me when I learned to give it to Jesus and trust Him completely.

This seems so simple, so easy to understand, but I cannot pretend that I always turned things over to

God so easily. I had to learn to take my problems to the altar, one by one, and leave them there.

Give, and It Will Be Given

When we give something to God, then go back and reclaim it, is when we really worry. So many times I did that. How often I laid my children on the altar, then picked them up and dragged them away and tried to carry them and care for them myself. I'd always have to take them back to Him again, and lay them at His blessed feet.

The lesson is, whatever you give will be given back to you. When you give encouragement, you'll receive encouragement whenever you need it. Give of your substance, and your children will never go hungry. David the psalmist said, "I have never seen the righteous forsaken and his seed out begging bread."[3]

These are the things God was teaching me in those years when I didn't know what He wanted to do, how I would provide for my children, and how we could buy that little house. He was teaching me that there is a seedtime and a time for harvest, and that whatever we sow, so shall we reap.[4] Whatever we sow, whether it be money, a smile, kindness, love, giving of our substance . . . whatever we plant, we shall reap.

Before God taught me those things, I always thought that seedtime was the natural sowing process in the spring, followed by reaping a harvest in autumn. But the heavenly harvest consists of sowing the gospel and reaping souls for Jesus. It means preaching the Good News of the cross, so a harvest of souls can be set free from sin.

When God's people get serious about sowing, when the cross is preached and the blood is preached and the message is preached that sinners can be set free, those seeds will bear a great harvest. When ministers of God earnestly begin to sow the seed of the pure gospel of our Lord and Savior Jesus Christ into the hearts of men and women, this nation shall see a harvest of salvation such as we cannot imagine. God is faithful. His seeds always bear fruit.

Preparation

Those two years I waited on the Lord, I stayed in prayer and often wept before Him. They were years of testing and held many trials; I am convinced that the devil constantly brought circumstances against me to try to make me return to the things of the world.

But Jesus knew I loved not the world or the things that were in it. As I waited on God, clung to Him, learned to trust and obey Him, the devil gradually released his grip on my life. However, you can never cease your vigilance: If you rebuke and reject the devil, you can count on his attacking those near to you, those you dearly love . . . particularly your children.

You can count on Satan to touch and wound your heart, to try to make you lose faith in your prayers, especially those prayed-for loved ones. For years on end, he will try to tempt you into discouragement and unbelief. Are you being tested? Is the enemy coming against your family? I learned to look up, to keep my eyes on Jesus. Oh, it's hard not to fix our eyes on circumstances when our very home and loved ones are under attack, but that's the very time we dare not look at circumstances.

Again and again Jesus told me, "Fix your eyes upon Me. Follow Me. Stay close to Me." I thought that was so beautiful, for He is the Way, the only One who knows the way in which God wants me to walk. Follow Him.

Cleansing the House

Then came a time in the early seventies when I was singing in a South Carolina amphitheater and saw someone aiming a television camera at me . . . a big camera. I didn't pay much attention, but when the program was over, the nice young man approached me and handed me his card.

"We have a Christian talk show, and would like you to be our guest," he told me. I didn't even know there was such a thing as Christian television, but I took his card—Jim Bakker, PTL, Charlotte, North Carolina, it said. I said, "Thank you," and wondered, *What is a talk show?*

Back in Nashville I laid the card aside and forgot it until the day Jim and Tammy Faye Bakker called and asked to schedule me on their show. *Oh my,* I thought, *I don't know if I'm supposed to do this or not.*

There was a reason why I wasn't sure. For several years during my backslidden period, I had gotten into astrology. It was during those years when I was searching, and I guess the devil got into the act and attempted to abort my search for God. A friend had my chart drawn up, and I read every forecast I could find. People in the music industry began to give me little trinkets with my astrological sign on them—teacups and paperweights and stuff.

I had a bunch of those objects in my house back then, and yet I was still miserable. Looking to astrology to give you peace and answers for your life is one of the world's biggest fakes. It gets you in so deep, and leads to severe depression. There's no answer in all that; there's no satisfaction for the soul.

After I rededicated my life to Jesus I never fooled with astrology again, but I still had the zodiac jewelry and trinkets and such, still had them in my house. One day when I was dusting, I picked up my Bible and it fell open to where God calls such things an abomination and warns us to give them up.[5] We are to have no false gods. So many of us need to cleanse our houses.

The moment I read those scriptures I gathered up all the dishes and trinkets and anything else to do with zodiac signs, things laying all over my house, and packed the whole lot into a pillowcase. I went outside and beat it against the sidewalk. "In the name of Jesus, I renounce everything that's ever come into my house that has to do with astrology," I cried out. "I denounce every false god that has come into my home. In the name of Jesus, I plead the blood of Jesus over my home."

I just beat that old stuff up and dumped it in the

trash can. Having renounced Satan's deception, now I was thinking about that invitation to the talk show. *Lord, what is a Christian talk show?* I wondered. Would I go there and find deception? At last I decided to go, but I would be very cautious.

Once there, I sat in the waiting room in an old building that had once been a furniture ware-house—this was in the very early days of the PTL ministry—waiting, listening, and wondering what I was supposed to do. I was trying to discern what this was all about, but I did know I would be talking about Jesus.

As I waited, I began to hear people in the back praying and praising Jesus. I noticed the Christian counselors. *They were praising Jesus.* Then the young man I remembered, came out and introduced himself. "I'm Jim Bakker, Betty Jean," he said. "The program is about to start, and we just want you to let the Lord have His way with you. We want the Spirit of God to move. Whatever the Lord wants to do, we want to be open to it."

My fears lifted. *Christian television is just fine,* I thought. Jim and Tammy Bakker were wonderful to me, and I returned to their studio many times after that, always praising God for the prayers that went up from there, and the many souls that were won to Christ.

I loved Jim and Tammy Bakker. I love them today. They were my introduction to Christian television.

Jesus, You're All to Me

So I began to venture out, as the Lord led, always happy to sing the songs of Zion that flooded through my heart, always wishing I could do more of it. At that early stage I would not have believed the direction in which God was leading me even if you could have told me. I'm glad I had no idea.

You see, so many Christians begin to minister before they are ready. Pastors and others in authority sometimes open doors to celebrities before they have had adequate time to wait upon the Lord, before they are spiritually ready. They may be a big star, or a name everybody recognizes, and because we live in the age where television and entertainment are glorified, I think we sometimes exalt these children long before they are ready to speak the things of God.

To be recognized in the world does not necessarily make a person full of God's wisdom. God is not interested in our popularity and talent; in fact, He doesn't need our talent. He needs our submission to Him so He can work in our life and work through us so that people may be saved.

Meanwhile, as those who are not ready often find pulpits waiting, others who are not known but are anointed of God, are not invited. I'm not impressed with movie stars, country singers, great sports figures, politicians, and all the others. God is no respecter of persons. He is not interested in how well we perform before the world, but in who we are and what we are. He is interested in the message our lives proclaim.

As I was to learn, God can take the least of us and use us for His purposes if we only will yield our lives and hearts to Him. He can even take a little mountain girl like me out of a life of heartache and loneliness, a life filled with deception, and carry her from her private dream world into His blessed reality.

That reality is Jesus Christ, and Him crucified. Bless His holy name!

Endnotes
1. John 14:6.
2. Psalm 50:10–12.
3. Psalm 37:25.
4. Galatians 6:7.
5. Deuteronomy 18:9–12.

Until You've Walked With God

VERSE 1:
You may have walked where kings and rich men traveled;
You may have lived where poor men can't abide;
You may have walked upon earth's scarlet carpet;
But you haven't lived until you've walked with God.

CHORUS:
Until you've walked that road that leads to heaven,
And seen the home He has prepared for you;
Until you've felt the joy of His forgiveness;
You haven't lived until you've walked with God.

VERSE 2:
You may stand in the lights of fame and honor,
And hear the vain applause of sinful men;
When all those things have failed to bring you comfort,
The answer's clear, you must be born again.

—BETTY JEAN ROBINSON

14

Until You've Walked With God

As Joe Johnson said, I needed to sing a different song. Now God was telling me the same thing; it was time to turn away from the old and do something brand new. But what would that be? For two years I prayed, questioned God, sought His face, and learned how to listen to Him. He began showing me different roads to take, different songs to sing.

I wrote some new songs during that time. Many of them contrasted my old life, with all its sorrows and failings, to the new peace and joy I was finding. For example, God gave me peace about turning down those major Nashville songwriting and recording contracts and even those that were big. I simply couldn't understand why at the time, bad as my family needed the money. I only knew I must obey God.

When you finally lay your talents on His altar, you dare not take them back. When I said "Yes" to God—"If I never sing again I will serve You for the rest of my life"—the glory of God opened up to me, and His angels ministered to me. He handed back to me all I had offered Him—and far more.

God doesn't need our talents, but He does need our commitment. Jesus wants our commitment, our whole heart.

As I yielded more and more of my life to the Lord, yearning to know Him better and serve Him more, I felt God wanted to show me something awesome. I began to feel His anointing.

God's Voice in a Dream

Sometimes God speaks to me in dreams. In a wonderful dream I had back then, people from all parts of the world streamed down the road in front of my little mountain home and crowded into the yard. In my dream flowers bloomed everywhere—roses, daisies, and violets . . . oh, a multitude of violets. They say violets represent friendship.

In my dream people stood everywhere under our redbud, maple, and dogwood trees, admiring the beautiful deer which come down off the mountain to eat the ripe persimmons that fall off the trees. Even the sweet little fawns aren't afraid to come close. The chipmunks were darting in and out of the old stone colonial fences on my property.

The people in my dream, all gloriously happy, were enjoying the little creatures. The foxes in our woods were there, and every kind of bird flew overhead. Beside every tree on our mountain a candle burned bright. I believe the Lord was showing me that one day people would be happy, and encouraged, and blessed by the songs from Melody Mountain, and many would see Jesus, the Light of the world.

I held that precious dream in my heart, though I could not imagine how God would bring it into reality. Once I had fine houses, good cars, and trivial pleasures. Now it was exciting to be invited to sing at some small church or Christian meeting. Sometimes I barely had enough gas in my old car to get us there, and after they'd give me a little offering so that I could buy gas for the car and stop for a hamburger or scrambled eggs on the way home. The Lord was teaching me to depend entirely on Him.

Paul and Jan Crouch

Then I began traveling all over the United States with an evangelist, singing at his tremendously crowded meetings in many of America's large cities. In the late seventies we flew to a revival in California, my first visit there. That's where I was introduced to Brother Paul Crouch and his wife, Jan, who at that time were pioneers in Christian television.

Their ministry had started out in the same small television station where they invited me to be a guest on their program. I liked Paul and Jan, and recognized their sincerity—that they coveted lost souls and had a tremendous vision for Christian television.

But that day I never could have dreamed of all Paul and Jan Crouch and I would eventually experience as we served God together in many different times and places. Then California seemed like a strange country, fast-paced and intimidating. My country songs had been played on the radio there, but California seemed like a different world.

I thought, *These are proper people and they might not like my country-sounding gospel songs, my old-fashioned "Amazing Grace," "Just a Little Talk With Jesus," and "Take My Hand, Precious Lord."* But when I sang "Amazing Grace" those fears just dropped away. The anointing of God was on it.

TBN invited me back to the *Praise the Lord* show— over and over again. Then came the day they began holding meetings at the Anaheim Convention Center. On one Sunday that auditorium, which held thousands of people, was packed out twice. God blessed Paul and Jan's vision, their faith, and their hard-working ministry.

As I walked out that first time to sing, my heart filled with feelings of inadequacy and deep doubts about singing to the multitude of "proper" California people. I had never sung to such a huge gathering before. What would they think of my old-fashioned singing?

I sang "How Great Thou Art," that Scandinavian hymn everybody loves. I had recorded it many years earlier with my own special touch. At that time, for some reason, I had asked a friend to help me translate one verse of "How Great Thou Art" into Spanish. Now I sang the verse to that packed-out auditorium of people, feeling a little embarrassed at my hillbilly version of Spanish. *It sure must sound funny to those folks in Anaheim,* I was thinking, when suddenly God showed me something amazing.

In a far corner of that great auditorium about a thousand Hispanic Christians had stood to their feet, lifting their precious hands to heaven and worshiping God. At that very instant, my eyes opened. I thought, *It's all right, I can just be me in California. I can sing what I love and believe in.*

During those next months, God allowed me to return many times to serve with Paul and Jan Crouch's ministry. Those California saints, the little grandmothers who anointed the grounds with oil, the people who covered those meetings with their prayers. . . . A great move of God had begun, and we were all involved.

But oh, the devils that fought against Paul and Jan Crouch's ministry in those early days—and still do—trying to destroy the vision God gave them, their vision that Christian television would someday go out across America and into all parts of the world. How the enemy hates that and continually fights against everything they attempt for God.

Obedient to the Vision

During those early years, men of God like Brother Jerry Bernard, Brother Kenny Foreman, and Brother Dwight Thompson would "preach down heaven" over those meetings and on those television programs. From that first little Christian TV station the

Crouches established, the couple continued to be obedient to their heavenly vision, and Paul Crouch has done what God has shown him to do.

Station by station, into Phoenix, then Seattle, into Florida . . . leapfrogging across America, crisscrossing our continent and moving far beyond, their vision has grown.

I had been placed by God where I could see and participate in those amazing events. I saw God move across America with miraculous speed, saving and healing countless thousands of His people, then moving overseas and into the far-reaches of this old earth.

Today Paul and Jan Crouch's Trinity Broadcasting Network, which has been built entirely debt-free (Paul Crouch refuses to borrow and pay interest on God's money), has more than five hundred cable television stations that carry the gospel around the globe. The Christian songs I wrote and recorded and sang to Jesus have gone around the world through those blessed stations, to many tribes and nations.

Sometimes I kick against the pressures that can come—the days and weeks away from home, the tiring travel schedule—but I've not given up because God has never given me peace about leaving Christian television. In fact, in 1983 He confirmed that I was supposed to remain where He placed me.

Up on Melody Mountain

One day in 1983 Paul Crouch asked if I'd like to have my own TBN program. If so, he wondered, could I give him some idea of what it might be like? What would I name the program? What would it contain?

"I believe I'd name it 'Up on Melody Mountain'," I told him. "I'd go back to people's roots, remind them where they came from. I'd reach out to those who once grew up on farms or in little towns, the ones who went to small churches, who maybe got busy with their lives and left Jesus behind. They left Jesus out of their lives. I'd want to reach back and remind them of their early days."

I'd always thought that I'd love to take a camera and go into different parts of the United States to interview God's people, to let them testify. The Lord knew my strength would not hold out, that it would not be the best way for me, so it was a desire that could never come to fruition.

Now here was this opportunity, and years earlier God had given me the theme song. Soon after I moved into my little house, I had written about how dark my home had been when I was a backslider, but now I had come to Jesus and our home was filled with His light. *Lord, You have come into my house and done a beautiful thing,* I thought. My old house had been filled with depression, and everything was gray. But when Jesus shined His light in, suddenly the sky turned blue, the trees, grass, and flowers full of color.

Suddenly I could hear the birds, even the little honeybees that come to the apple blossoms in my orchard. The deer, raccoon, and red foxes, all God's creatures that I watch from my window and back porch. . . .

"My life is full of light, each room full of bright-ness, and each day full of happiness up on Melody Mountain. That's what the song tells," I explained to Paul Crouch and his TBN vice president, Terry Hickey.

"That's what we have in mind for you," they both agreed. "That's what your program needs to express."

"Lord, what am I going to do with a thirty-minute program?" I began to ask God. "I can't teach, I'm not a preacher, so what are people going to expect? Will they even *want* to hear me? I'm nobody." I really came down hard on myself.

Meanwhile, TBN assigned me a production studio and set up production. Doug Marsh, a precious, tal-ented young man, built the set according to my ideas . . . the same set I've used all these years. I gave Doug some magazine clips to illustrate my idea of a pretty country house, filled with homey things—and he created it.

When the day came to go to Oklahoma to produce my show's first pilot film, my voice totally disap-peared. Seated in the old van with my clothes packed inside, I sat with my head bowed, crying out to the Lord.

"Come on! Your flesh is fighting this thing so hard, it must be the Lord's will," my friend said. So we started the old vehicle and headed out to begin the program I felt terrified to start.

That's the way "Up on Melody Mountain" came into being. Every time I spoke on that program, I directed my words to those who were hurting. It was as though I could see them through the camera's eye . . . terribly lonely and abandoned. The Lord would direct me to speak to the prisoner, the sick, or the brokenhearted.

The message was for broken people who thought God could never hear them. It is God's will for such forgotten people to be lifted up, to be encouraged, to be brought to salvation.

As the years went by I wrote more and more songs of comfort, songs that pointed people to Jesus. During my years with Trinity Broadcasting Network I have simply ministered as the Lord leads me.

How I love to sing, and how richly God has blessed me. He has carried me far beyond anything I could ever dream, and yet there's more to tell. Much, much more.

VERSE 1:
It's been a long year, Lord, yes I've had some pain,
Seen a whole lot of sunshine, felt a whole lot of rain;
But I've got Your promise, Lord, there's sweet victory,
So whatever You're doing, keep working on me.

VERSE 2:
Been up on the mountain, no comfort my soul,
When I'm poured out like water, I know I'll come forth like gold;
Then I'll soar like an eagle when You set me free,
You know what You're doing, Lord, so keep working on me.

CHORUS:
Keep working on me, Lord, keep working on me,
The fire's getting hotter, Lord, so many tears I can't see;
Oh, but You know what You're doing, Lord, and I know it's good for me.
So I'll hold on to You, Jesus, while You're working on me.

VERSE 3:
Now you don't tell the Potter what to do with this clay,
It's His own good pleasure, oh, to have His own way,
Like you did for ol' Stephen, just show Your sweet face to me,
And I'll be all right, Jesus, while You're working on me.
—BETTY JEAN ROBINSON

15

Keep Working on Me

Even before I went to TBN, God sent me into many little churches. At first I had to borrow a car from a friend who owned a car lot, but of course we couldn't keep doing that. Then a evangelist gave me a beautiful old car that held up for a while, and the Lord provided the next one, and all the others since.

Remember, I was being tested. *Will you go? Will you go without provision?* I would trust the Lord, and the people would take up a little offering for me. I always got back home safely. God never fails; He always provides.

Melody Mountain Music

Tests come to the greatest of saints as well as to the

least. If we will say yes to the small things, God can trust us in the larger responsibilities. By the late seventies after much prayer, I became bold enough to go to the bank and borrow four thousand dollars to set up my own record company—the Melody Mountain label. After turning down offers from the big companies, this seemed like the low road to take, but the Lord had a reason. So did I; I knew I needed to hear from Him, and that I should not be in covenant with anyone else.

That bold step on my part enabled me to cut a record all the music experts *knew* wouldn't go. My first gospel recording on the Melody Mountain label, titled "Songs I Grew Up On," featured the old songs: "Will the Circle Be Unbroken," "Shall We Gather at the River?," "Take My Hand, Precious Lord," and others I knew from childhood.

"Contemporary music is what's happening," everyone told me, but I listened to my heart. Today, years later, that first Melody Mountain record is still selling, and so are all the others. They have had no promotion; I had all the hype that I wanted when I was in the world. I turned my back on that. I wanted to sing, write, and record songs that touched people's hearts. I just wanted to glorify Jesus. I still do.

Songs kept coming to my heart, and I kept writing them down. I felt strongly about these new songs; I wanted to write for my own company and not be under contract with the outside music world. Little by little decisions, some big, some small, had to be made.

Keep Working on Me

Songs Heard Far and Wide

In the early eighties God spoke to me during a church service in Phoenix, Arizona, saying, "I am the Lord thy God who healeth thee."[1] Soon after I came back home to Melody Mountain, for some reason I turned on the radio in my kitchen and heard Brother C. M. Ward preaching. "There's going to be a song written this year that will be heard far and wide. It's going to bring glory to God," he said.

I wonder if I could do that, I thought. *Maybe I could write a song like that.* Then I got scared, wondering if I was getting full of pride. I put the thought out of my mind, afraid pride was entering there. I told myself, *No!*

A few days later I was in my kitchen when God spoke to my heart, saying: "I am Jehovah, the God that healeth thee." Straightaway I picked up my guitar and sat down at my kitchen table. I've written so many songs there, sitting at that table with my guitar. The moment I sat down and struck an A-minor chord, I began to hear God's words in my mind, God bragging on Himself, because only He can.

He said, "I am Jehovah, God of creation; I am Jehovah, Lord God Almighty; I am the balm of Gilead. I am the Rock of ages; I am Jehovah, the God that healeth thee."

I started singing, and the song began to pour into my soul. As I rejoiced the words kept coming out: "I am the great I Am; the God of Abraham."

As I hit the minor keys on my guitar I could hear

this sound, this Israeli sound, a sound that came as I let the Lord move upon me. He said, "I am the great I Am; the God of Abraham; Jehovah, Shalom, the God of Peace; I am the God of Israel; the everlasting Arm; I am Jehovah, the God that healeth thee."

By this time I was caught up in the music, praise music pouring out of my soul, and I rushed on; "Sing hallelujah, sing hallelujah, sing hallelujah. I am Jehovah, Lord God Almighty; I am Jehovah, the God that healeth thee." And the song continued, "I am your provider, Jehovah-Jireh; God of salvation; God of Messiah. My Son who came to you, and testified of Me. I am Jehovah, the God that healeth thee."

Oh, I rejoiced and rejoiced. How my soul did rejoice as the anointing rested above the kitchen table as I sang, and that song was birthed in me. A few days later I wrote another song, "Messiah," about Jesus, and a few days after that one I called "The Comforter Is Come."

Many of my songs were recorded by fellow Christians as the years went by. Brother Jimmy Swaggart recorded "I'm Livin' Up on the Mountain, and I'm Alright" during the years when his ministry was covering so much of the earth. He recorded "Let Down Your Net," and "Wade in the Water, He's Pouring Out the Latter Rain." And because he ministered to me during those years, I felt so appreciative.

Brother Kenneth Copeland recorded "The Comforter Is Come," and "He Is Jehovah," and I just rejoiced. I never knew that song would be heard far and wide, as it has been. But I know that in my times of walking with God in the deep valleys, when

Keep Working on Me

"Jehovah" was being sung in many different places in the country, sometimes I would lie down with a heavy heart. But all at once I could hear that song being sung somewhere.

Sometimes I would hear Kenneth Copeland sing it far away, and people were rejoicing and praising God. That song would waken me out of a sound sleep and I would laugh in the Holy Spirit, just laugh and rejoice. The Lord was letting me rejoice, and all my heaviness would be lifted. I would fall back to sleep like a baby. The Lord is so good. He has ministered to me in song, and I want to share His songs with His precious people.

Co-Laborers in God's Vineyard

I purchased a little piece of land from Brother Dillon Sullivan up on Melody Mountain, where everything we needed would be right there. We built a small barn on that new land, fashioned after a certain barn I'd seen on the countryside. Using barn plans from The Home Depot, we turned the barn into a small three-story base for operations, built partially over a hollow, so Melody Mountain laborers would have a pretty view of God's country.

One beautiful day in 1985 Pastor Sullivan, a carpenter by trade, presided over the cornerstone ceremony there on Melody Mountain, having placed scriptures inside the stone. We chose Psalm 37 and Matthew 16:18; ". . . upon this rock I will build my church; and the gates of hell shall not prevail against it."

These scriptures were sealed inside a little New

Testament and set within the cornerstone of our ministry building. We gathered together, Pastor Sullivan and the rest of my sainted co-laborers, and we dedicated our ministry to the glory of God with prayer, praise, scripture, preaching, and songs.

As the prophet had said to me, "God says you are to build your foundation on a solid rock." That rock, our Cornerstone, is Jesus Christ, our blessed Lord and Savior.[2] Praise be to God!

Endnotes
1. Exodus 15:26.
2. Matthew 21:42.

CHORUS:
Anything that brings you closer to Jesus is good for you;
If you're looking in God's direction, don't change your
view.
Any old road you might be walking, any trial you're
going through,
If it's bringing you closer to Jesus, it's good for you.

VERSE 1:
If your troubles are bringing you closer to Jesus,
Well, just praise His name,
For when you touch the hem of His garment,
You're never gonna be the same.
You're gonna shout hallelujah when the light of His love
shines through,
For anything that brings you closer to Jesus is good for
you.

VERSE 2:
Every heartache and every frustration that comes your
way,
Tell Jesus about it in your conversation when you kneel to
pray.
Every invisible mountain you're climbing, every valley
you're walking through,
If it's bringing you closer to Jesus, it's good for you.
—BETTY JEAN ROBINSON

16

Anything That Brings You Closer to Jesus

My daughter needed a great healing. Elizabeth Kimberly was twenty years old and three months pregnant with her first baby when she went to the doctor for a checkup, and he called her to come back to his office right away.

Her husband was at work, so I went with Kimberly to the doctor's office. "There are cancer cells in her womb," he told me, "and we'll have to take the baby. We're going to have to decide soon. What do you say about that, mother?"

Lord, have mercy, I thought, shocked at the news. But fear didn't overtake me. I reflected over the many times I'd seen God heal, the times He had touched my body, the times in the mountains when we'd watch Brother Lankford lift a tiny, sick baby up to Jesus. He'd say, "Here it is, Jesus," and Jesus would heal it.

Yes, I had seen miracles, and I thought, *Lord, I might as well say it right now.* "Doctor, Jesus is going to heal my daughter," I told the doctor.

He looked at me as if I were crazy, got very angry, and said, "I don't believe in that. You discuss that stuff outside the office, but not here."

We left the doctor's office, came home, and anointed Kimberly with oil. The Bible tells believers to anoint the sick with oil and pray, and that is all we knew to do, that and wait for the manifestation of healing from God.

It takes a lot of faith when someone says your child has cancer cells in her body. Certain words like *cancer* put fear in someone's heart. We can believe God can heal a headache, but we wonder if He can heal cancer. *This is a deadly disease, Lord.*

The Divine Physician

But Jesus is the Great Physician. He knows every cell in our body, because He made them all. What more could we possibly need? He told us, "If thou canst believe, all things are possible to him that believeth."[1] Now I don't know why some are not healed, while others are. We don't know those things, because they are in God's hands.

But we're told to have faith, realizing that He is the Great Physician and knows all things.[2] By faith my sister Martha and I, and several other saints, prayed for Kimberly and believed for her healing, and that of her babe. A couple of weeks later Martha and I and several other friends sat in my living room, just talking about the Lord, worshiping Him, and singing songs, when Elizabeth Kimberly came in and laid down on the couch, where she fell asleep.

Kimberly had accepted my faith in the Lord. She simply accepted my decision to tell the doctor we'd go home and trust Jesus to heal her. As Kim dozed, others quietly went home until there was nobody else in the room but Martha and me. My sister and I continued to sit there in the presence of the Lord in the still of the evening.

It seemed as if a breeze blew through that room, blew the curtains, and blew through on us. A silence fell over Martha and me, so that we couldn't speak. We sat there in awe, realizing that the presence of God had filled that room. We were afraid to move. When the Lord reveals Himself, in His greatness, often you are afraid to move and just want to sit and bask in His glory. How wonderful He is!

Martha and I felt God's spirit sweep past us in that room as He went to Kimberly and laid His healing hand upon her sleeping body. At that moment she became totally healed as the fire burned out every cell that was an imposter in her body. Praise His holy name!

As Martha and I meditated there, still speechless with holy awe, Elizabeth Kimberly suddenly arose from the couch and placed her hand on her stomach. "Mama, I felt a hand of fire touch my stomach," she told me. "Something has touched me." Then my child began to break out in perspiration and became very thirsty. She went to the refrigerator and drank a whole lot of ice water.

Martha and I both believe that when Kimberly felt what she described as "fire" touch her stomach, at that moment Jesus touched her, just as He did when He said to the little girl who had died. "Maiden, arise."[3] When that child arose from her deathbed, Jesus told her mother to give the girl something to eat. When my child arose up from the couch, she was thirsty and began to drink water.

There Is No Other Fountain

A few months later, Hadassah was born, the baby the doctor had suggested must be aborted so Kimberly could live. But thanks be to God, Kimberly is living and so is Hadassah. I named the baby, giving her the Hebrew name for Esther. One interpretation of the name is that of the myrtle tree, the tree of healing.

How I thank God that we trusted Jesus. For us, He came and healed Kimberly. During those days in which we waited to see His healing manifested, I wrote a song called "There Is No Other Fountain." I was driving my car one day, when all at once I began to sing: "I will draw my strength from Jesus as I lay upon His breast, I will take from Him my comfort, I will find in Him my rest. For there is no other fountain where I can be more satisfied, than in the arms of my sweet Savior, no blessing will I be denied."

The second verse says, "All pain will leave my aching body as His sweet healing virtue flows, and demons tremble in His presence; in Jesus' name they have to go. For there is no other fountain where I can be more satisfied, than in the arms of Christ my

Savior. No blessing will I be denied."

Straight Into the Arms of Jesus

Sometimes it's the most painful things of life which draw us to Jesus. *Cancer,* that terrible word, is no blessing, but I believe even cancer can be used for good when we let it bring us close to God. Things too painful for us to bear are so often the way the Holy Spirit brings us into the presence of God, who is all we ever need, no matter how deep our suffering, pain, or loss.

Things that drive us to our knees—a drowned baby, fear, loneliness, a faithless husband, great financial need—can take us straight into the arms of Jesus. Yes, bring your sorrows, heartaches, and pain to Jesus, but first bring *yourself* to Him. Tell Him you are a sinner, that you are failing, that your life is a mess. Ask Him to forgive your sins, come into your heart, and change you.

There is a time and a place for each of us. God is present in every circumstance of our daily lives. Jesus waits for us just beyond the tragedy, the scary events, and the heartbreak. Seek His face. Seek Him now.

> But God commendeth His love toward us, in that, while we were yet sinners, Christ died for us. Much more then, being now justified by His blood, we shall be saved from wrath through Him (Rom. 5:8–9).

That is God's promise to every man and woman

on earth who will believe the gospel.

Endnotes
1. Mark 9:23.
2. Mark 2:17; 4:34.
3. Mark 5:41.

The Shade at the End of the Row

VERSE 1:
Tall Kentucky mountains, green Kentucky corn,
A picture of my old Kentucky home;
Hot sun on my shoulder makes me want to go
To the shade at the end of the row.

CHORUS:
I can see the heat waves dancin' on the dusty ground;
See my old sleepy hound dog, Billy Joe,
See Daddy wipe his tired old brow and lay his hat down
In the shade at the end of the row.

VERSE 2:
June bug in my pocket, red worm on my line,
The fishin's good where the piney river flows;
Kentucky sun keeps shinin', sure makes me want to go
To the shade at the end of the row.

VERSE 3:
Now Daddy's gone to heaven, he laid his old hat down,
Hot sun don't shine on his back no more;
His work down here is over, and Jesus took him home
To the shade at the end of the row.

VERSE 4:
I can see my daddy down by the riverside,
Resting where the peaceful river flows;
Daddy, I'll be coming soon, and we'll sit down and rest
In the shade at the end of the row.

—BETTY JEAN ROBINSON

17

The Shade at the End of the Row

That song paints a picture of a mountain man. It's written to my daddy. But to tell of Daddy's salvation, baptism, and death you'd have to sing of the love and mercy of our everlasting heavenly Father.

My daddy, Dewey Rhodes, was a hard-working, stubborn, honest man. He loved his children, but once he whipped me and in my humiliation I drew back from my daddy who I loved so much. I went on loving him, and he loved me, but I was never again as close.

Then I grew up, moved away, and grew even farther away from my daddy. As you know, I also grew far away from God. My own story seems like a parable of how even God's children—who know Him and love Him dearly—can still move away, grow cold, then backslide.

The story of my daddy and me, and my precious Lord and me, hold many similarities.

Oh there was no hatred, no real unforgiveness, just the silent barrier of fear that made me stay distanced from Daddy. He may have wondered why I never talked to him very much. Mountain people don't say "I love you" very easily. We act out our love in our deeds and our service to one another. Never did my dad or stepmother tell me in words that they loved me—and oh, how I yearned to hear those words—but they trained me, taught me, and sacrificed for me. So I always knew my daddy loved me very much.

Then came the day in 1970 when I got word that Daddy had taken extremely ill in his lungs. He had the black lung disease, but turned out one lung had turned cancerous and must be removed. His condition was so serious they called his children to the bedside. As I traveled toward my childhood home, how I regretted not making things right with my daddy, and how I prayed I'd get there in time!

"Well With My Soul"

Daddy wouldn't let nobody but our Martha Belle take care of him. Martha, my tender-hearted little sister, the one who always takes care of everybody, asked our daddy before his surgery, "Is everything well between you and God?"

"Daddy, you have not gone too far that you can't come back," Martha told him. "Jesus loves you, and

The Shade at the End of the Row

He's still got His hand outstretched, waiting for you to come home." Daddy was a good man, the son of my little Holiness Mammy and our Baptist Pappy, but he never went to church. He sent us children to church, but he wouldn't go. We knew there was an important step Daddy needed to take.

Soon we could see Daddy in the intensive care unit, tiptoe in one by one and whisper to him. When it was Martha's turn she said she saw peace all over his face. He took her hand, and said in his little raspy voice, "Martha, everything is well with my soul. While I was asleep under that anesthetic I heard the most beautiful singing I ever heard in my life.

"It wasn't of this world, Martha. It was like the angels of heaven. It was hundreds of voices. And you know what they were singing? 'Hold to God's unchanging hand. Build your hopes on things eternal, hold to God's unchanging hand'."

Martha said she immediately thanked God in her heart, praising Him that He is so big He can go down to the very depths of man's soul in that spirit realm, and that He would speak to our daddy's heart so Daddy would return to Him. How we praise God today that our daddy was saved for eternity! Daddy had been a backslider for so long.

Clear Creek Baptism

From that day forward, Daddy's life was completely changed. He'd sit on the front porch during the next months, the eight months before he died, telling all who'd listen about the wonderful things God had done for him. As he grew weaker, his every breath harder and harder to take, as happens with that old black lung disease, Daddy wanted to be baptized, to do his first weeks works over—for there had been a time in the distant past when he had belonged to a church.

By now Daddy was so terribly sick, but they took him to Clear Creek, up there in that beautiful cold water, and my Daddy waded out in there with the preacher from Mount Hebron Baptist Church who baptized him. I was not there to witness it. Betty Jean Robinson was back home in Nashville, writing country songs, far from God at the time. How I wish I had been like Martha, ready and able to point a lost soul toward his salvation.

Before Daddy died I came home to visit. How he witnessed and talked to every neighbor who came to visit him. How he would cry and wipe the tears from his eyes with his little old handkerchief as he testified that he'd been such a bad person, but now God had saved his soul.

He testified at the Mount Hebron Baptist Church while I was there. He said, "Come with me," and I followed him down the worn aisle of that little wooden-floored church to the altar, him with his white handkerchief, and he started patting that foot to get the rhythm, like we do in the mountains. We knew when to clap hands and how to pat feet right, because that rhythm comes from inside.

And then Daddy was singing, and me with him, "Time is filled with swift transitions . . . Hold to God's unchanging hand." He kept singing it at the altar

The Shade at the End of the Row

there, and it was an awesome moment.

His words touched me. One time I went out on the porch and Daddy said, "Sit down and sing, Betty Jean." He said, "Sing, 'When I walk up the streets of gold, the burdens of life may be many and the frowns of the world may be cold, but to me it will matter but little, when I walk up the street of gold.'"

I sang to Daddy, observed the change in him, knew that my daddy was saved and ready to meet his God, but I was still backslidden and far away from Him myself. Before I returned to Christ, I wrote a song that described our daddy and his mountain existence, a song that paints a true picture as far as it goes, but without the wonderful hope my daddy now knew firsthand.

Shotgun Road

VERSE 1:

Daddy used to work in the big coal mine on Shotgun Road,
And everybody lived like they's never gonna die, on Shotgun Road.
Then the sad day came and the mine shut down,
Sealed that shiny black coal in the ground,
Now all they got to do is get up and lay down, on Shotgun Road.

BRIDGE:

Oh, Lord, have mercy on Shotgun Road.

VERSE 2:

Daddy used to walk with his head held high on Shotgun Road.
He made a good living and we had a lotta pride on Shotgun Road.
Yes, my daddy once walked with his head held high,
Now he don't care if he lives or dies,
And Lord, have mercy, when the children cry on Shotgun Road.

VERSE 3:

Well, what'cha gonna do when the bread's all gone on Shotgun Road.
Poor little children skinny as a bone, on Shotgun Road;
What'cha gonna do when the bread's all gone,
Shoot a cottontail rabbit, give the dog the bones,
And try to be thankful you still got a home on Shotgun Road.

VERSE 4:

Everybody talks about goin' up north on Shotgun Road,
And Ollie Mae Baker said everybody ort', on Shotgun Road.
Well, we may go today, and we may go tomorrow,
But who wants to jump from the skillet to the fire,
And anyway Ollie Mae Baker is the liar of Shotgun Road.

VERSE 5:

So we plant a patch o' popcorn out behind the house on Shotgun Road,
And sit around and try to watch a cat try to catch a mouse, on Shotgun Road,

The Shade at the End of the Row

Go behind the house and plant a little patch o' corn.
For Lord, it's trouble all day long, on Shotgun Road.
—BETTY JEAN ROBINSON

Yes, my daddy knew so many sad times in his life, and now he was dying. *But he had Jesus!* He had his eternal salvation. He would see his Pappy and Mammy in heaven. He knew that, and he could rejoice.

They called me home before he died. He was in that room in the hospital where they put those who are going to die, that old death room, where an old intruder—the death angel—waits. But if the death angel was waiting in that room, I believe there were also angels of the Lord waiting to carry Daddy to heaven.

When I got there he couldn't speak. He struggled so hard to breathe, it was terrible. I stood there, helpless, and a little Pentecostal preacher slipped into the room, knelt beside Daddy's bed, and said, "Lord, give Mr. Rhodes peace."

I saw peace sweep over him. He could even breathe better. And I began to talk to Daddy, open up my heart to him. I told him that I loved him. I got to tell him that before he died. Thank You, Jesus.

Home to Straight Creek

That July 1970, they carried his casket up to Mount Hebron Baptist Church up there on old Straight Creek. Brother Theo Carter, who was like our spiritual father, one of the old-time preachers of the faith, preached Daddy's funeral. As Brother Carter preached about heaven, we knew our daddy was there. As I sat looking out the window, studying the world outside, the saddest thought came to my mind. *Daddy would pass our little four-room house on his way to the grave. He would never return there again.*

We buried him on the side of our beautiful Kentucky mountain. That day in the church, I thought: *How sad that the funeral procession will pass the little garden Daddy worked, where he plowed with that old mule and raised the food we ate. He will pass the place where his children grew up. . . .*

But now I see far more clearly. I know my precious Daddy will rise one day with Pappy and Mammy and all our loved ones who have gone on to be with the Lord. On that day our beautiful mountains will resound with the shouts and praises of all the saints we have known, and those who came before them. Hallelujah!

On Silver Wings

VERSE 1:
*There's a resting place where you can go
On silver wings from the world below,
When trouble comes, lift your voice and sing;
You'll be lifted up on silver wings.*

VERSE 2:
*On silver wings you'll take your flight
From your longest days, from your darkest nights.
There's sweet release from temporal things,
When He lifts you up on silver wings.*

CHORUS:
*On silver wings you'll be lifted up,
Renew your strength, refill your cup.
Lift up your eyes, raise your voice and sing,
You'll be lifted up on silver wings.*

VERSE 3:
*On silver wings there's a resting place,
Where you can look on the Master's face,
Where you can bathe in the healing stream;
There's perfect peace on silver wings.*

—BETTY JEAN ROBINSON

18

On Silver Wings

On His silver wings, God lifts me above every valley and helps me soar high over stony mountain peaks. Through my program on TBN, the churches far and wide welcome my ministry, through all the dear co-laborers in the vineyard, and all the precious pastors . . . those wings lift not only me, but every other child of God. He shows us His awesome majesty and glory.

I love God's dear saints, and I love doing His work on this earth. Over the years we have ministered to thousands and even millions; men on death row, women in prisons, people who are ill or old or helpless, addicts, those in pain, people without hope.

God has allowed me to write hundreds of songs about Jesus, so many songs I can't count the number. We sow songs like seeds from across Melody

Mountain to as many as will ask, seek, or write, people in all parts of the world. God Himself will bring the harvest.

Those silver wings carry me in person and via television to far-flung places on this earth. Sometimes they carry me forward, but often they carry me back . . . back to my beginnings, back to my earthly heritage, and culture. Now that I travel and minister for God, I have come to a deep appreciation and thankfulness for those who came earlier, those who ventured into our deep, dangerous mountains where outsiders never dared to go, America's pioneers of the gospel, come to bring light to places where men's lamps often flickered and died.

Reunited

And now that I reach people of many different cultures—South Africa, Haiti, Canada, Alaska, Europe, and Mexico, to name just a few—God has taken me back to my own Cherokee Indian roots. In recent years He has called me to minister to the Indians— both those above our borders, called North American Indians and those within our borders, the Native Americans—where God has reunited me with two powerful cultures.

The first includes some of my physical bloodline; such tribes as the Ojibwa and the Cree in various locations in Canada; or the Tulalip, Crow, Flathead, Blackfeet, and Pawnee tribes within our borders. The wonder of God's taking me to these beautiful, worshipful people, often so isolated, yet so connected to the land, the physical world, of their fathers!

In these places people often gather to attend Christian meetings in the dead of winter, traveling miles across the frozen wilderness, hungry for all God has to offer. At times I fly into Canada in someone's small plane and get out in howling winds, snow whipping our faces, and the temperature fifty degrees below zero. There stood my precious brothers and sisters ready to take us to the reservation to feed us a wonderful meal before we begin our worship. We always have wonderful fellowship together.

The Native American and North American Indians love nature, but they do not worship nature; they worship the One who created all that beauty. They do not take beauty or any other good thing for granted. I look into their faces and wonder about my little part-Native American mother, Annie Gray. I think of her grandfather, Gray Wolf, who changed his name to Glenn Gray, who decked his horse with beautiful feathers and loved our Appalachian Mountains, and who knew and loved God and could preach the gospel.

I think of my young girlhood, when I felt so different from the others, so sad and set apart. Now at last the Lord God has set me among some of my own, where something in our hearts seems to recognize one another, and give me such feelings of peace. I know I will see Annie Gray in heaven; I will meet my mother there, and Gray Wolf, her Holiness grandfather, and the many others of their people whom I already love. Meanwhile, God has sent me to many tribes, to love each person there.

A Dove in the Mountains

Such worship! Again, it's like coming home, home to our mountains, back to Straight Creek where we walked the railroad track to Brother and Sister Lankford's house for an evening of prayer, praise, and worship, sometimes surrender, sometimes repentance and weeping, or sometimes a return to the Lord.

Like my precious mountain people, these Indian people hunger for God. They want holiness. They believe God's Word, seek Him in their daily lives, and practice the things of God in their homes, villages, and individual lives.

From these reservations, I believe we shall see revival fires begin to spread. Here is the humble spirit, the plain lifestyle, the seeking after truth, and giving up all the ways of the world. And these people see miracles—old-time miracles of deliverance and healing. They know God's power firsthand and depend on Him for their needs.

Long ago in the Appalachian Mountains of Kentucky, Virginia, West Virginia, and North Carolina, another move of the Holy Spirit empowered some of America's most poverty-stricken and helpless. The dove flew across the mountains and lit upon so many people who were so poor, and the blessed outpouring has lasted unto this day.

Jesus came to people with sad eyes, tattered clothes, and empty lunch pails. He came to the poorest of the poor, the destitute. Around the turn of this century, men came in on horseback, usually two by two, riding into this obscure country where so few people lived. These men had received the baptism of the Holy Spirit and sometimes had been put out of their denominational churches because of this blessed gift.

So the zeal and the fire were in their bones, and they were led of the Holy Ghost into the mountains, especially to the area where we lived. The men would ride until they saw a house. They'd follow the light in that hollow, go to the house and ask to spend the night. Often no one in that house was saved. As the visitors knelt to pray before bed, the people in the home would realize that God was with them.

Before the travelers left that location, as our old people still testify, in many cases blind eyes were opened and men with tuberculosis were healed. People lying under old quilts on their iron bedsteads which were pulled close to the fire would be healed, often after lying there sick for years. They'd see that surely the Lord had come, and they'd kneel down and pray, giving their hearts to God.

In that way, God made flaming swords out of so many of those mountain men. And when the wind of the Spirit begins to blow, men are caught in it. They just flow with that wind, because there's a hunger within them, a desire for God. And when that wind blows, people lay down their plows and shovels to spend time with God. Women forget about their home duties and concerns and spend time worshiping, praising, and praying.

There's a hunger for God at such a time, and it's

the most important thing there is. People long to be satisfied; they seek God the way the psalmist tells it, "As the deer pants for the streams of water, so my soul pants for you, O God."[1]

Then comes the singing. You could hear them as they went about their work; you could hear people in the mountains singing as they went into the mines. You could hear them in the fields, in their gardens as they hoed the 'taters. They'd sing as they milked the cows or hung clothes on the line. The songs rung out over those mountains. What a sweet sound, and oh, to hear it again!

I am describing revival, children, revival like my precious Native American friends are praying will come over our nation and our world. Revivals that would last for three, four, or five weeks, where children went to church every night, and the men came from the coal mines and the fields, hurried to feed the stock and wash up, then walked miles to church. Sometimes they walked through the doors as they tuned their old guitars. The song service would be started already when many walked in.

I can see the little pickup trucks with straight chairs set up along the sides in the back for people to ride in, with little children sitting at their feet. Riding to church, going to every service to see what God was going to do. Hearts so hungry and yearning to know what God would do.

Brother Theo Carter told how in the old days men ran across the mountain from Tennessee into Kentucky where there revival was happening. The men traveled from county to county, praying and worshiping God and praying for the sick. Some ran thirty miles across Cumberland Gap, and weren't even tired, not even out of breath, when they got to church.

But persecution followed the Pentecostal baptism. Often the churches were burned and the people threatened. When the wicked would slap these saints in the face, they would turn the other cheek.[2] Following what the Bible told them to do set the believers apart; they were called "Holiness folks." There were accounts of people who mocked the saints, burned their churches, and hurt the saints of God, but as a result these mockers met death themselves, and very swiftly. Often the sinners shunned those who chose what we called "the good way," the way of holiness.[3] There is a price to pay for following Jesus.

An Unquenchable Fire

Revival fires cannot be quenched; they are the fires of the Holy Ghost, which burn forever. They burn away the dross and make us humble. Like the little mountain Baptists and the Holiness folk, we can wash one another's feet. And if you have aught against your brother, you cannot bow and wash his feet and still hold anything against him in your heart.[4] You can only love him.

I can remember that at Brother and Sister Lankford's house, no one left without kneeling and praying with Brother and Sister Lankford. If you came to Brother Lankford's house sick, he would pray for your healing. I'd often sit down in an old cane-bottom chair, and Brother Lankford, with his old overalls and his white shirt buttoned up to the top button, would get the oil. He would stand behind me and pray as he poured oil in his big, rough coal-mining hands and then rub it on my forehead.

After all these years, I can feel those blessed rough hands as he ministered to me and prayed to our God. "Sis," he'd say, "I like to pray for you because there is no obstacle there. When I pray for you it goes right on through my hands."

When the doctor told Sister Lankford she had cancer on her tongue, that precious saint who always worshiped Jesus believed He would heal her. Oh, the nights I would hear her praising God from her room. She'd kneel by her bed way into the midnight hour, calling out to God. And one day, Jesus touched her tongue. She was totally healed.

I could go on and on. As I travel, minister, and pray for another mighty move of God, He continues to bear me up on His silver wings. My heart ponders the blessed simplicity of my Native American and mountain heritage. My heart yearns for the fullness of my Holiness heritage. I long to be described by that old mountain term for a woman who chose "the good way." Mountain folks would say, "You can't spot her life."

That's what I yearn to see God do for America. May America turn back to the good way, and may her people desire to be without spot. I praise God for His great and mighty works, which He has privileged me to see. I praise God for His saints, and those the Holy Spirit will yet apprehend. And I praise God without ceasing for the holy fires of His revival, which He is kindling today in Native American reserves, on the plains of Africa, in the mountains of our nation, and upon every other place in His world.

I come from an obscure place and from little-known people. But God knew me by name from before the foundation of the world.[5] He knows you too, and loves you with an everlasting love.[6] Let Him bear you up on silver wings. Amen.

Endnotes

1. Psalm 42:1, NIV.
2. Matthew 5:39.
3. Isaiah 5:35:8.
4. Matthew 5:23–24.
5. Ephesians 1:43.
6. Jeremiah 31:3.

Epilogue

Papa, Mammy, my mother Annie Gray, and Daddy are in heaven with the many old saints who touched my life. Hala still lives in our old home place on Straight Creek. She is nearing eighty years old.

Lucy Mae and Martha Belle have lovely daughters and grandchildren: Dean, Linda, sister Christine, Cynthia, and Martha are my co-laborers in the Lord's work here on Melody Mountain. My half brother, George, has two sons: Michael and John Mark. He lives on Straight Creek.

Harry was found dead from a heart attack just outside his company office years ago. It is still so sad for Rebecca, Elizabeth Kimberly, and I. I pray he found peace in his soul. I have five beautiful grandchildren: Sunday, Joshua, Rachel, Hadassah, and Annie.

From my memories to you . . .

LOVE,
BETTY JEAN

About the Author

Betty Jean Robinson was born in the Appalachian mountains of Kentucky. From an early age, she was constantly exposed to the richness of country music and old hymns of the faith.

It was Betty Jean's grandmother (or "Mammy" as she affectionately called her), who instilled a rich Pentecostal Holiness legacy within her. And Mammy's efforts and prayers weren't in vain. At thirteen years of age, Betty Jean came to know her beloved Savior and Lord, Jesus Christ, as the power and the fire of the Holy Spirit burned within her.

During her senior year in high school, the Federal Bureau of Investigation (FBI) in Washington, D. C., hired her as a typist in the Fingerprint division. The fast pace of city life eventually lured Betty Jean away from her first love—Jesus Christ. During her years working with the FBI, Betty Jean met her husband, William Harold Robinson (or "Harry" as she calls him). They fell in love, married, and had two daughters, but Betty Jean longed for her Kentucky home. While Harry provided for all their needs, he neglected the most important part of life—his family.

Betty Jean began her songwriting out of the loneliness, pain and sadness in her own heart. Ironically, her songwriting was the very thing that led her to country music stardom. She soon became a songwriter for country artists such as: Connie Smith, Porter Wagner, Charlie Pride, and Hank Snow.

But Betty Jean's Holiness roots tugged at her to come home. At the pinnacle of her music career, she retreated to her mountain home for two years while seeking God's direction for her life. She began using her musical talents for God's kingdom, writing Christian songs including "He Is Jehovah," "On the Way Home," and "Jesus Is Alive and Well." Later, God would lead her to Christian television at the time when Paul and Jan Crouch were establishing the Trinity Broadcasting Network (TBN). God has flourished TBN and, as a result, Betty Jean's program, *Up on Melody Mountain,* is seen regularly by millions around the world.

Today Betty Jean lives in her mountain home in Straight Creek, Kentucky. She enjoys being with her two daughters, Rebecca Lynn and Elizabeth Kimberly, and her five grandchildren: Joshua James, Sunday, Rachel Hala, Annie Gray, and Hadassah.

If you enjoyed *Up on Melody Mountain,*
we would like to recommend:

Help! I'm Raising My Children Alone
by T. D. Jakes

Are you lonely and discouraged? Are you afraid for your child's future because of your painful past? T. D. Jakes offers help and hope for single parents and for those who sometimes feel like they are. From his own personal experience being raised by a single parent and with anointed biblical insight, Jakes shows you how to "be loosed" from the perils and pitfalls of living in a broken home.

Passion for Jesus
by Mike Bickle

Have you ever wondered how God feels about you? If you could get just a glimpse, you would become a new person. *Passion for Jesus* will help you see the passion and splendor of God's personality. It will help bring you to personal wholeness and spiritual maturity and will awaken in you a fervent devotion to God.

All in God's Time
by Iverna Tompkins

The road to our purpose in life, whether in our ministries, our careers or even in our relationships, has been mapped out in ways we often don't understand but God does. If you have ever wondered when your road to royalty will end, then this book will encourage you to await, with patience and joy, the day of your coronation.

Available at your local Christian bookstore or from:
Creation House
600 Rinehart Road
Lake Mary, FL 32746
1-800-283-8494
Web site:http://www.strang.com